Stewardship economy   3

land, environment and climate

Julian Pratt

Published by

Lulu.com

Editorial note

This book brings together previously unpublished material which
Julian worked on alongside the summary book, *Stewardship
Economy 1: private property without private ownership*. With the
other five books in the series, it provides the additional material that
lies behind the proposals and assertions made in book 1.
Unfortunately, aspects of this work are unfinished, some of the
examples provided are out of date, there is some repetition of text
and some references (bibliography in book 7) are not available. I
hope you, the reader, will excuse this and will find the work as a
whole thought-provoking and topical.

Rosemary Field

September 2021

ISBN 978-1-4717-0255-6

Contents

Stewardship Economy

The **Stewardship Economy** series of books questions one of the foundations on which market-based economies rest: the system of property rights. It suggests that the form of private property that works well for the things that we make is both unethical and inefficient when we apply it to land and the rest of the natural world. It proposes an alternative to ownership – stewardship.

The underlying principle of stewardship is that everyone is entitled to an equal share of the wealth of the natural world. The steward of any part of the natural world has the secure and exclusive right to use it, the responsibility to care for it and the duty to compensate others for excluding them from it.

In practical terms this means that stewards of land pay fees that are equal to its market rent. These fees provide revenue that may be used to provide government with an income that is an alternative to orthodox taxation and, ideally, to provide everyone with a (small) Universal Income. Stewards of environmental resources pay fees equal to their resource rent, and this revenue is distributed to everyone as an Environmental Dividend.

Books in the series

Stewardship Economy 1: private property without private ownership is the first book and provides an overall summary of the main ideas.

Stewardship Economy 2: Valuing land and managing transition sets out in some detail how to establish the market rent of land and how to make the transition from an ownership to a stewardship economy. It also considers how the revenue from stewardship fees might be distributed.

Stewardship Economy 3: Land, environment and climate (this book) explores how a stewardship economy would transform the way we use land, provide housing and develop our cities. It goes on to consider how stewardship would help address pressing environmental and climate concerns.

Stewardship Economy 4: The economy, wealth and universal income focuses on the impact of stewardship on the national and global economy, how the distribution of wealth would be changed and the impact of a Universal Income.

Stewardship Economy 5: efficient, fair taxes and the role of the state describes the some of the adverse effects of our current system of taxation and considers the role of the state in a stewardship economy. It also explains some basic economic principles and terms.

Stewardship Economy 6: property rights describes the systems of property rights in our current economic system, their history and how property rights could be more fair and efficient in a stewardship economy.

Stewardship Economy 7: some economics explained, economic terms and bibliography. This book provides an introduction to some key economic concepts for the non-specialist and lists the references, as far as they are available.

Introduction

Part I of this book explores how a stewardship economy would transform the way we use land, provide housing and develop our cities. Chapter 1 describes how land is used in ownership and stewardship economies. Chapter 2 explores the significance of the planning system for land values in an ownership economy and for stewardship fees in a stewardship economy. Stewardship brings geography into economic thinking and has important implications for cities and regions. These are explored in Chapter 3. Chapter 4 explores the impact of stewardship on housing provision and Chapter 5 considers how a stewardship economy would affect the way we manage the countryside.

Part II goes on to consider how stewardship would help address pressing environmental and climate concerns. Chapter 6 looks at factors that influence the way we manage our environment; chapter 7 considers how amenities and resources are managed in an ownership economy vs. a stewardship economy; chapter 8 looks at pollution; chapters 9 and 10 explore the contribution of stewardship to addressing climate change and sustainable energy production and chapters 11 and 12 look at how a stewardship economy can increase efficiency, sustainability and fairness in management of the natural world. The book concludes in chapter 13 with an account of the new enclosures, the global commons movement that is growing in response to concerns about climate change, and how stewardship may be compatible with this commons.

The full bibliography is in book 7.

Part I   Land use, cities and places

Chapter 1 Land use

Some land is used intensively while other is used hardly at all. It will sometimes be a matter of opinion whether land is overused or underused but when we look around a city and see sites that have been boarded up for years, or houses that are empty and decaying, it is clear that there is something wrong. The planning system plays a part, but the root cause is the nature of ownership. Would we make better use of land in a stewardship economy?

Ownership economy

Hierarchy of property rights

In the UK freehold property rights in land are held from the crown and people who use the land may find themselves at the end of a series of leaseholds.

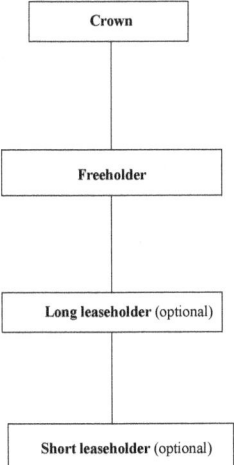

Private property, collective (state) property and common property may all be held as either freehold or leasehold.

A system of private property is organised around the idea that something belongs to an individual or legal entity. This 'belonging' confers on the owner the capacity to determine the use to which the property is put. Collective property (state or public property) applies where the use of resources is determined by reference to the intent of the collective as a whole. No one individual makes decisions about the use of collective property without reference to this intent. Collective property, in high-consumption economies (as opposed to low-consumption, 'developing' economies) is usually held by the state, by some tier of government or its arms-length agents. Common property is a third alternative and refers to property rights that are held and managed by a defined community of commoners. It is similar to collective property in that no individual member of the community has specially privileged access, but different in that those who are not commoners are excluded, and the collective has no right to be consulted.

Over-investment in land

Land is treated as an investment asset just like shares or commodities. The economy suffers because any investment that is made in land is not invested in productive economic activity. Often and is not used efficiently because it is held by those who want to invest in it, rather than by those who want to use it. Like the investor in gold bars, investors may be content to watch their investment lie idle in the knowledge that it is safe and unlikely to fall in value in the long run.

Under-use of land – the extent

Since 1990 Scotland has published an annual survey of vacant and derelict land compiled from returns by local authorities (Scottish Government 2008). In 2007 this amounted to over 10,000 hectares (25,000 acres – a hectare is 100 metres by 100 metres) without including agricultural land, land in settlements of less than 2000 people and sites of less than 0.1 hectare.

In England in 2005, almost 31,000 hectares of land (0.2 per cent of the total area) were recorded as derelict or vacant in the National Land Use Database of Previously Developed Land, along with a further 22,500 hectares that were in use but considered to be underused or in low-value use and to have development potential.

Centre Point, the iconic 1960s London office tower, was notoriously kept empty for 15 years after its completion. Patrolled by guard dogs, it was known as the most expensive kennel in Europe and reached full occupation only in 2009.

Under-use of land – the causes

Sometimes land is held out of use because a developer is engaged in the time-consuming process of acquiring a number of connected sites or putting together finance. Land may lie idle for other reasons, including planning delays and the challenge of rehabilitating degraded land. But the nature of ownership and the structure of the financial system ensures that there is remarkably little incentive to put land to its full use, and even some disincentives.

The planning system can be slow and tortuous, particularly when a development is contentious or where it involves a Site of Special Scientific Interest (SSSI). Some of this is due to the understandable complexity of the issues and the necessity for democratic control and transparency. But much of the delay is avoidable. The planning system is discussed in more detail elsewhere (Chapter 2).

Degraded sites may be expensive to rehabilitate, particularly those that suffer from contamination, flood risk or ground instability. These may require some form of subsidy to return them to a condition in which they are an asset rather than a liability.

Taxes on property (land plus buildings), including in the UK council tax and national non-domestic (business) rates (NNDR), are levied on both the land and the improvements (buildings). NNDRs are in part a tax on the market rent of the land and in part a tax on the rental value of the buildings and other improvements upon it. The tax on buildings and improvements discourages development by reducing the value of the completed development, thereby reducing the optimal use of land. This is exacerbated by the approach to valuation of the property in its current use. If the property were to be valued on the basis of the highest and best use (HABU) to which the property could be put under current planning regulations, this would provide an incentive to optimise its use. If taxes on land amount to less than its market rent, the incentive to make the best use of land (subject to planning regulations) is below optimal.

Taxes like the council tax and the NNDR are deliberately reduced in many circumstances where properties are underused. Council tax is paid at a lower rate where there is a single occupant. The aim is to make housing more affordable to single people, but the effect is to promote under-use of properties. The most extreme example of tax reductions for underused properties occurs when a property is empty. Properties are exempt from council tax for the first six months during which they are unoccupied, an improvement on the earlier limitless exemption. Properties are fully exempt from NNDR if they are too derelict to be used, as their value at current use is zero. The effect may be that viable buildings may be destroyed, de-roofed, gutted or otherwise made uninhabitable in order to avoid payment of property taxes that have become unaffordable.

Ownership may disguise the cost of under-use, for example, if a firm rents land from a landlord at a commercial rate, this market rent shows up in its business accounts. If the land is owned outright, its imputed (notional) market rent (the cost of the opportunity lost by failing to rent it to somebody else) does not appear when the accounts are drawn up on a cash basis. Accruals accounting, in which there is a charge to expenditure for the economic cost of capital assets, would be required for the purchase cost of the land to show up in a firm's accounts and even then is not as compelling as actual payments of rent. Where a firm is too small to use accruals accounting, or where the charge to expenditure is an underestimate, a firm may under-utilise the land in a way that they would not if they were renting. Jarsen (2003:40) found that public limited companies that own their own premises are less successful and have lower sales than those that rent premises. The ratio of their stock market valuation, a measure of their profitability, to the book valuation of their assets is also lower – which also suggests that these assets are not being used well. When a company behaves in this way, and a predator recognises that its assets could be more profitably employed, it lays itself open to an asset-stripping takeover. Ownership does not in the long run benefit owner occupiers of firms.

An important incentive for owning unused and under-used land is the expectation that its market value will rise. Land values have tended to rise over the last 200 years and superimposed on this, are cyclical fluctuations. This means that, during the upswing of the economic cycle, land prices rise very steeply. When this happens, landowners do not want to sell today, or even to rent on a long lease, because they expect that land values will continue to rise. Owners may also delay selling even when land prices are static or falling because they remember previous land price increases and expect that the time will come for prices to rise again.

The biggest gains in land value, up to 200-fold, occur when planning permission is granted for agricultural land to be used for residential purposes. There is a powerful incentive to hold on to land if there is any prospect that planning permission may be granted in the future. It can even be in a developer's interest to allow land to become derelict as this wears down local opposition to an application for planning permission.

Land banks may lie idle for decades. The ostensible reason for this is that a developer needs to be able to bring one project on stream as another is completed without being delayed by having to acquire land, obtain planning permission and so on. The possibility of profiting from rising land values may also, no doubt, contribute to the developer's thinking. There have been suggestions, too, that the major supermarket chains have used their land banks to deprive competitors of the opportunity to open new outlets. Land ownership is a form of local monopoly and provides the basis of many business advantages. Fred Harrison (1983:67) cites a study showing that land at the edge of six metropolitan areas in North America was transferred from traditional rural owners to investors and developers some 15 years before the land was developed for urban use.

Expectations of rising land prices, and the low direct costs of owning land (particularly when held out of productive use), work together to ensure that the underuse or non-use of land is frequently a prudent financial decision. In this context the behaviour of land speculators, who buy land with the principal intention of selling it at a higher price is rational – if at times risky. If land is held off the market in the expectation of a price rise, the problem is not the behaviour of an individual landowner acting in their own self-interest but the nature of the land ownership system. Overt speculation, though dramatic, is probably a less important cause for the under-use of land than the speculative tinge that affects most land-use decisions and valuations.

Even where there are willing buyers and sellers for land, the market is inefficient There is a lack of comprehensive and publicly available information about both the true sale price that was paid for each site at its most recent sale) and the extent of land currently available for sale.

In summary, ownership economies have inefficient land markets characterised by inadequate information, speculation and financial incentives to leave land derelict and under-used.

Stewardship Economy

Hierarchy of property rights

In a stewardship economy a Stewardship Trust is the ultimate proprietor. It may be a self-organised commons trust, a state body, a private sector body holding a franchise from the state, or a not-for-profit body permitted by the state. Most stewards are individuals or corporate bodies that hold private property rights from the Stewardship Trust, but some stewards are state bodies holding collective property rights from the stewardship trust, and some are groups of commoners holding common property rights (Stewardship Economy: Book 1).

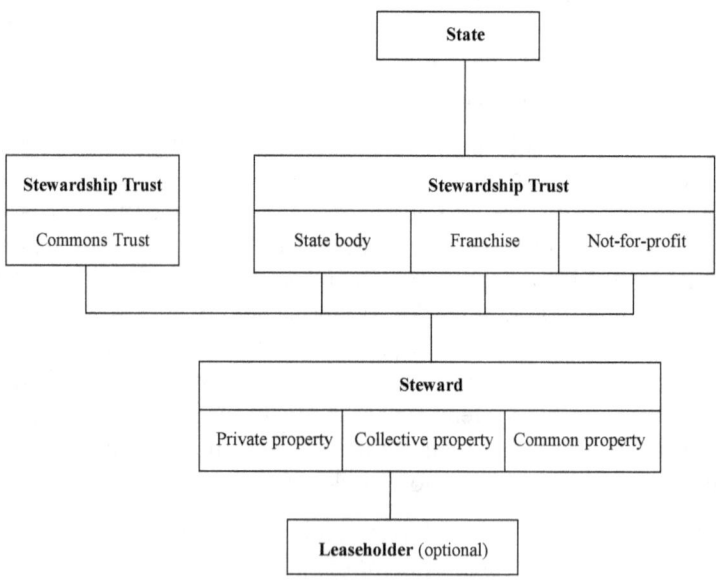

Role of the steward as landlord

In a stewardship economy, the steward of unimproved land derives no income (net of stewardship fees) from leasing it to a tenant. This means that unimproved land ceases to command any future expected rents and so has no market value. There are no benefits for being a landlord who simply rents out unimproved land but where there are improvements, such as a house or a factory or a farm, a landlord can continue to play an important and profitable role in a stewardship economy by owning, maintaining, developing and leasing the improvements to a tenant – just as a hire company might lease out a car.

In a stewardship economy it seems likely that there will be fewer people leasing and renting land, and more people who are stewards of the land they use themselves (steward-occupiers). For this reason, plots – particularly of agricultural land – are likely to be smaller, and there will be more of them. People using the land may be more likely to care for it, and put it to better use, than would absentee landlords.

Stimulating development

Stewardship fees are due whether land is in use or not which encourages the steward to put it to the best possible use permitted by the planning system, whether by carrying out some enterprise on the land, leasing it or by deriving satisfaction (utility) from using it. The financial penalty for underuse of land, arising from the payment of stewardship fees on all land, makes more land available for those who want to put it to use, whether for housing or business. This puts a downward pressure on market rents. In addition, as the market value of land is zero it does not function as a financial asset and so there is no rationale for speculative landholding.

Land Value Taxation has never been deployed in a way that captures a high enough proportion of the market rent to realise the full extent of its potential economic benefits, though Land Value Capture using other approaches has proved very effective in Hong Kong, Singapore, and Latin America (Stewardship Economy: Book 2). It has proved difficult to uncover credible evidence of the impact of Land Value Taxation on local property development, but what evidence there is suggests that it has a neutral or beneficial effect on new building (Richard Dye & Richard England 2009:8).

While evidence of impact is lacking, mathematical modelling of Land Value Taxation demonstrates that it leads to early development of all sites, with all land put to productive use. If it is assumed that all buildings have an indefinite lifespan, therefore, development will be locked in at low density levels. High density land use is less easy to establish than would be expected, thereby distorting the pattern of land use (Richard Arnott & Petia Petrova 2002:30). This provides a reminder that it is important that there should be no barriers to the constant redevelopment of sites, which can be achieved if the value of improvements is adequately depreciated (Stewardship Economy: Book 2).

The term 'split-rate taxation' is applied to a system of local property taxation that is a sort of half-way house between a Land Value Tax falling on the land only and a conventional property tax falling equally on land, buildings and other improvements. It applies a higher rate of tax to the land than to the improvements, and so does not penalise new building as much as does a conventional property tax. Fred Harrison (1983: 195) describes case studies of split-rate taxation in the Australian state of Victoria between 1966 and 1978. Cities applying a split-rate tax experienced more rapid sales of vacant sites, and a greater number of new dwellings, than cities applying the same rate to buildings as to land.

Pennsylvania is the only state in the USA that allows municipalities to tax buildings and land at different rates. Pittsburgh and Scranton adopted split-rate taxation in 1913 and a further 17 cities adopted it between 1974 and 1994. Florenz Plassmann and Nicolaus Tideman (2000: 218) report that all these 17 were at the outset in economic distress, with empty downtown areas, and hoped their tax reform would stimulate building. Several studies had shown no correlation with increased construction, but, by accounting for the statistical distribution of building permits they were able to show that between 1972 and 1994 the cities using split-rate taxation had significantly greater levels of construction than cities using the same rate for land and buildings. Tony Vickers (2007:51) uses their figures (Florenz Plassmann & Nicolaus Tideman 2000: 241) to estimate that in Pennsylvania, a 1 per cent shift in property taxes away from the buildings and onto the land is associated with a 16 per cent increase in construction.

Urban sprawl gives rise to transport and other infrastructure requirements that are themselves costly and environmentally damaging. It is unconducive to social cohesion, unattractive and a waste of space. Development in a stewardship economy would take place more readily and more rapidly and undeveloped plots would be rarer, urban development more compact and infrastructure costs lower.

Traditional forms of taxation cause some business sites to be unprofitable. If we imagine an economy without taxes, land in Figure 1 ranges from highly productive on the left to unproductive on the right. The land that is shaded dark is beyond the economic margin of production – it is not put to use because the return is not enough to pay the business costs including wages (the return to labour) and interest (the return to capital). 'Rent' refers to the return from the use of land, the annual market rent, and may be manifest either as a market rent paid by a tenant or as an imputed rent (see Book 6) in the case of an owner-occupier.

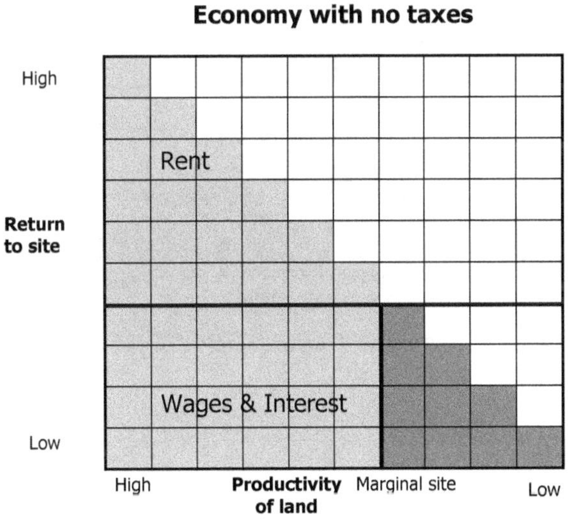

Figure 1 (based on Tommas Graves 2011)

Figure 2 shows the situation in which NNDR (national non-domestic rates) have been introduced, and all other variables such as planning conditions and GDP are assumed to be unchanged. Some sites that were previously used for production no longer generate enough return to pay the total cost of NNDR plus wages and interest. NNDR drives these sites out of use, and the margin moves to the left.

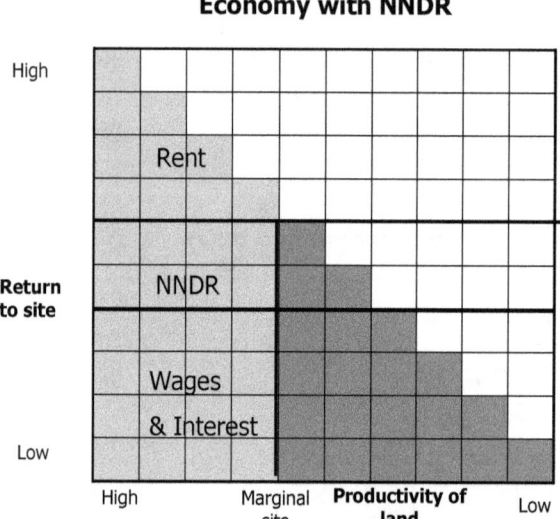

Figure 2 (based on Tommas Graves 2011)

Figure 3 shows LVT introduced in place of NNDR, and again all other variables such as planning permission and GDP are assumed to be unchanged. LVT falls less heavily on less productive land than on more productive land, and not at all on marginal land. The margin does not move and production continues at all the sites on which it occurred when there were no taxes.

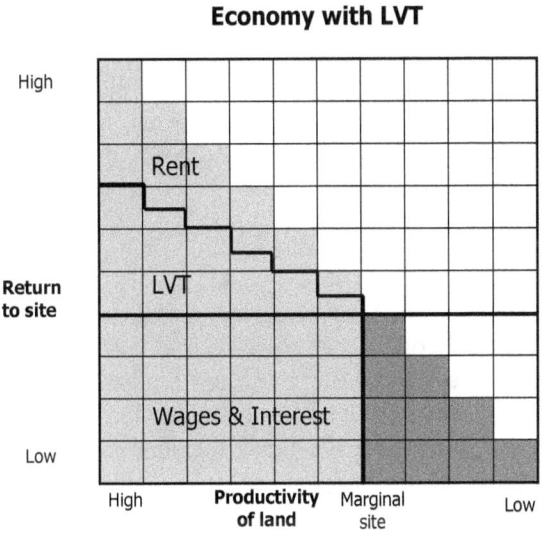

Figure 3 (based on Tommas Graves 2011)

Whereas conventional taxes reduce the amount of land that can support production, Land Value Tax does not. More land will be in productive use when subject to LVT than to NNDR, and this can be expected to support more people in employment.

As sites at the economic margin tend to cluster in areas of deprivation at the geographical margin, switching from NNDR to LVT provides an incentive for businesses to relocate from areas of high land value (for example south east England) to areas of lower land value. This stimulates the regeneration of deprived areas (Julian Pratt 2011; Ewald Engelen et al 2011:47). Other factors help with regeneration; a steward can develop land more easily as they have no need to borrow money for its purchase and there is a greater incentive to develop properties because there are no taxes to pay when new improvements are built. The combination of stewardship fees with a Universal Income transfers wealth from areas of high per capita land values to areas of low per capita land values. This provides everyone living in areas in need of regeneration with a greater income, which in turn stimulates the development of businesses and employment.

One significant risk of stewardship is that it could place an undue pressure on stewards to overdevelop their land, but this risk is reduced by the impact that stewardship has of bringing other land, particularly seriously under-used land, onto the market. However, the only reliable protection against over-development would be a robust planning system.

Although Land Value Tax is usually described as a reform to the tax-benefit system, which of course it is, the most significant aspect of a 100 per cent Land Value Tax (stewardship fees) is to change the nature of property rights so that they are conditional on the payment of these fees.

Automatic subsidies for land

The Land Stewardship Trust has the responsibility to care for the land and, if no steward comes forward who is prepared bid anything at all as stewardship fees for a site, the Land Stewardship Trust will normally allow negative bids. It allocates the land to whoever makes the lowest negative bid and pays them the amount of the bid (a subsidy called a Stewardship Support Fee) (Chapter 3).

Where land is used to provide a public good, such as a park or public space, it will rarely generate enough income to command a positive market rent. Provided that the planning authority prevents its development, only negative bids are likely to be made. These public goods receive an automatic subsidy from the Land Stewardship Trust.

If a site is derelict and in need of rehabilitation, the Trust will assess the extent of the disimprovements. This is the sum that the exiting steward will be required to pay to an incoming steward as compensation. The disimprovement value provides either an incentive to the current steward to carry out the necessary rehabilitation, or funding for an incoming steward to do so.

In summary: in a stewardship economy stewards face a cost of holding land, which brings several benefits:

- under-used land is put to use, reducing dereliction and urban sprawl

- the land market is efficient
- land prices are stable and land speculation is eliminated.
- This in turn makes land available at low cost to those who want to put it to use but are currently excluded from it.

Chapter 2   Planning

Would a stewardship economy lead to the overdevelopment of land? Could low-impact uses, that are environmentally and socially beneficial but generate little income, be sustained? This chapter explores what is needed for the planning system to play a vital and central role in a stewardship economy. First it considers some aspects of the planning system as it applies mostly from the perspective of the UK.

Ownership economy

Protection from overdevelopment

The land and wider environment have in many cases been protected not just by the planning system but by benevolent owners, restrictive covenants and conservation easements.

Some landowners, particularly the large, landed estates, have thought of themselves as stewards and have played an important role in the conservation and protection of land and the environment. Land and historic buildings have often been preserved for generations, isolated from market forces and the pressure to develop by the commitment of landowners to preserve their heritage. This preservation has, in effect, been subsidised by the sacrifice by the landowner of the difference between the market rent of the land (if it were put to the most profitable permitted use) and the rent the landowner receives in its relatively undeveloped state. We can be grateful for this largesse while fearful that future landowners may not be so generous.

Restrictive covenants are agreements that restrict the way in which land is used and developed. They are placed in the title deeds to a property and passed on to subsequent owners, enabling an owner's desires to be executed in perpetuity. Severe restrictions reduce the value of the site and they may be a way of perpetuating benevolent ownership. Conservation easements are a form of restrictive covenant is widely used in the USA. Regional or local land trusts (of which over a thousand are funded jointly by local charities and the state) make a cash payment to a farmer who places a conservation easement on their land that permanently blocks any further development. In this way the owner sells the development potential of the site to the land trust and the benevolence is provided by the land trust, while the farmer is able to realise at least some of the development value of their land without any change in land use.

The need for planning

The main way in which overdevelopment has been curbed in ownership economies, however, is the planning system. In the UK we have had planning laws for more than a century, stimulated by the impact of road transport on commuting and ribbon development. The 1947 Town and Country Planning Act reflected the same wave of post-war idealism that gave us health care free at the point of delivery and free secondary education for all. It radically restricted the ability of landowners to carry out development on their land, effectively nationalising development rights. It gave us Green Belts, national parks, the New Towns and a framework of high-level plans to provide accountability and transparency to local planning decisions.

Planning restrictions must be used judiciously; they limit the area and permitted density of land that is available for housing and commerce, push up prices and have the potential to reduce economic growth (Economist 4/4/15: 18). But they provide safeguards and prevent landowners (or stewards, in a stewardship economy) from acting without reference to the wider community. They represent a claim by society on the way the land is used and include restrictions on developments that damage the environment or destroy buildings, trees and other beneficial assets. They protect from development agricultural land, open spaces and Sites of Special Scientific Interest.

Green Belts, which have successfully reduced urban sprawl as well as providing amenity and ecological benefits, are under threat as a result of the demand for more house building and the potential capital gains by landowners when planning restrictions are relaxed. There are always calls to remove planning restrictions, supported by developers and landowners who will profit by their removal.

Rather than less control over development, however, we need better control. There are many examples of inappropriate developments, and anyone who wants to see the degradation of exceptional rural beauty has only to visit Donegal where lax planning regulations seem to have allowed the construction of a 'bungalow in every field'.

Calls to remove planning restrictions on greenfield sites are unconvincing in an economy where so many homes are empty and commercial buildings underused, and in which there have been only inadequate attempts to make poorer parts of the country more attractive to business and families. There are large numbers of undeveloped brownfield sites, though not all are available for development as some may themselves be worthy of conservation either as wildlife habitats or as accessible green spaces.

The need for a better planning system

The planning system appropriately imposes restrictions on developers, but there are plenty of examples where the process is inefficient and unduly prolonged. There are major challenges related to the imbalance of power between planners and developers, issues of accountability and the tension between local and national priorities.

Planning decisions are taken by local authorities, which have always been under-resourced and have recently been particularly stretched financially. The planning authority has the unenviable task of balancing the wishes of the developer with those of local people in the context of the needs of the local and indeed national economy. The potential financial gains for landowners and developers when planning permission is granted are so great that they can invest substantial resources in making planning applications and particularly in appealing against the decisions of local planning bodies. The planning authority needs to minimise its legal costs, and at the appeal hearing the developer's well-resourced specialist legal team of QCs may be arguing the case against a relatively poorly briefed and inexperienced local solicitor. This imbalance of power creates a democratic deficit.

Even at the level of an owner-occupier seeking to make improvements to their property, the potential gains to the landowner, financial and other, are enough to tip the scales against the planning authority. The owner-occupier may employ the services of an experienced planning consultant, often trained by and having recently left the employment of the planning authority, to argue their case. When a planning authority grants permission for development of a site, there is no guarantee that this will go ahead. The owner may be content just to see the value of their land rise without having to carry out any development. Planning is permissive rather than prescriptive.

The planning system has attempted to take into account the views of local people, but this has been overwhelmed by the imbalance of power already noted. One approach that had positive aspects is the way in which the Localism Act 2011 fostered the development of neighbourhood plans. This provided funding that allowed groups of local enthusiasts to draw up plans and to consult with the wider community. However, there were many criticisms of the process: that it was promoted to undermine and bypass local planning authorities; that it worked mainly in middle-class areas where there is more time and capacity for this sort of engagement; that it was dominated by small groups of self-selected activists who often took a narrow view of their local self-interest and that the resources have been channelled to private sector planning consultants. But it has given a new group of people the experience of spatial planning and consultation and some of the plans have been very thoughtful.

There may be tension between national and local priorities. Strategic issues need to be decided at a national level, with national politicians taking political accountability, while local inquiries need to consider whether a local site is suitable for a particular type of development.

Government proposals in 2011 included a presumption in favour of 'sustainable development' but interpreted this as an integrated approach with three components: planning for prosperity (economic), planning for people (social) and planning for places (environmental). This is in practice interpreted, not as sustainable development in the accepted use of the term but as prioritising economic growth over environmental and social protection.

Planning processes often serve to secure the rural environment for the rich and to exclude poor people from access. The understandable desire by planners to prevent rural sprawl is preventing the development of energy-efficient, low-impact homes and self-contained communities. The Town and Country Planning Association campaigns to ensure that the government upholds existing policy and ensures that land around towns becomes the site for a range of ecological and sustainable uses.

Simon Fairlie defines low impact development as "development which, by virtue of its low or benign environmental impact, may be allowed in locations where conventional development is not

22

permitted." (2009) Low impact development does not need to be subject to regulations that prevent suburban sprawl, and it could be provided at a cost affordable by people who work there. Research in low impact development and practical examples has led to an increasing acceptance of this option within UK planning policies.

Who bears the cost of public goods?

There are many places where residents recognise the need for new housing but are also aware of the damage that will be caused in their neighbourhood by increased traffic, crowded schools, visual blight and so on, and fear a financial loss if development leads to a fall in the sale price of their home. This loss may also occur when a development such as a prison or a wind farm goes ahead. In some situations, such as new roads, compensation may be available, but this is by no means always the case and is paid as a lump sum to the present owner rather than as a stream of compensation to those affected in the future.

An owner may resist the designation of their land as a site of special scientific interest (SSSI) because this would impose limitations and obligations on the use of the land and reduce the value of their property.

In summary: planning is essential to provide public goods, but it has too often been poorly resourced, slow and undemocratic. Planning decisions, intended to promote the common good, bring both unexpected costs and windfall gains to landowners. The planning system needs to involve greater local participation with different standards and flexibilities for low-impact rural developments. It needs to be better resourced, more proactive and prescriptive.

Stewardship economy

In a stewardship economy it is even more important than in an ownership economy that the planning process be thorough, fair, speedy and transparent because it affects both land use decisions and the fees that stewards pay. Stewardship places planning at the heart of the economy and enables it to determine (prescribe) land use rather than, at the most, simply permit it.

Planning structures

Planning bodies at a local and national level regulate the use to which each site may be put, and so set the parameters within which the Land Stewardship Trust establishes stewardship fees:

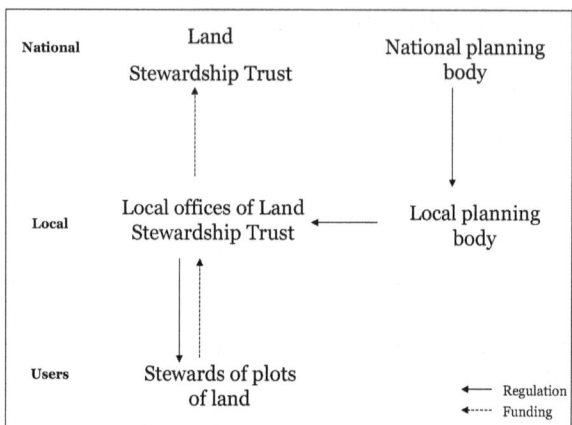

Planning bodies are accountable through the political structures at the level at which they operate. So, the local Land Stewardship Trust would be regulated by a local planning body which is accountable to a Local Authority, itself subject to the national regulator.

Enabling new development

Planning decisions are much more likely to be put into effect in a stewardship economy. Once planning permission is in place the steward has to pay higher stewardship fees even if they do not carry out the development for which the permission has been granted. This means that the steward is likely to go ahead with the development (or transfer it to somebody who will) so that it generates the income necessary to pay the increased stewardship fees. Planning in a stewardship economy is not just permissive but prescriptive.

Planning in a stewardship economy needs to balance protection of landscape and environment with enabling new development where this is required for social or economic reasons. It has much more opportunity to do so to achieve this balance in a stewardship economy, provided it is adequately resourced, because planning is prescriptive. More land is available than in an ownership economy and stewards have a financial incentive to put their land to the highest and best use permitted by the planning system.

Protection from overdevelopment

Benevolent owners, restrictive covenants and conservation easements are likely to play less of a role in preventing overdevelopment than they do in ownership economies. But although the impact of stewardship on a single site is to increase the pressure for development, when applied to the whole country it brings more land on to the market which reduces its market rent and makes this available for development too, thus spreading the development activity. Other factors that protect land from over-development include the increased attractiveness of areas of low land value for development, and the control exerted by the planning system.

The greatest pressure for development falls on the sites that are the most underdeveloped compared with the potential level of development permitted by the planning regulations. Bringing this underused land into development reduces the pressure for development on greenfield sites.

Stewardship reduces the level of demand for second homes and investment properties, as these are not appreciating assets. Another way in which stewardship may lead to less pressure for development is, for example, where the steward of a site applies for a planning decision to prevent the construction of new houses on their land in order to reduce the market rent of the land and the stewardship fees they need to pay. This contrasts with the current situation where the owner of a site normally has a financial incentive to apply for planning permission to develop.

Risk to sites currently not put to good use

Some people live or work in places where land is not put to its economically most efficient use, but these people nevertheless contribute to a diverse and flourishing community – for example people who live in a low-income low-impact way on the land, and businesses that are well-loved and contribute to the diversity of cities but are not very profitable. There is a risk that they might be driven away by the need to pay stewardship fees that are equal to the highest rent that anybody would offer for its use. To prevent this there is an even greater need for planning in a stewardship economy.

Stewardship makes subsidy by benevolent landowners difficult to sustain because they have to pay stewardship fees that are equal to the market rent of the land. Individual landowners would find it difficult to provide this gift indefinitely but if society values their contribution it could reduce their stewardship fees by imposing planning conditions that are sufficiently onerous to lower the stewardship fees or even render them negative – Stewardship Support Fees (Chapter 1).

The need for planning

The risk that stewardship could create undue pressure to overdevelop means that a fair, transparent and effective planning system is even more necessary in a stewardship economy than in an ownership economy. It is placed under intense scrutiny because the market rent of each site, and so the stewardship fees that have to be paid by its steward, depends on the planning restriction on the plot. The planning system lies at the heart of a stewardship economy, and one of its key roles is to protect sites that serve the community's best interests while not turning a maximal profit.

Restrictive covenants and conservation easements

Restrictive covenants and conservation easements reduce the market rent of land, and so reduce the stewardship fees that are payable on that property. There is a risk that they would be used as a means of tax avoidance. It is essential, therefore, that they cannot be introduced unilaterally by a steward but, instead, require review by the planning authority and be approved as legally binding only where, and for as long as, they are judged to be appropriate for the community.

Impact of Universal Income

The combination of stewardship fees with a Universal Income transfers wealth from areas of high per capita land value to areas of low per capita land value (Chapter 3), providing a subsidy to those living and working in areas of low per capita land value. This subsidy stimulates the economy in these areas and encourages people and firms to locate there, increasing demand in previously depressed areas and taking the pressure off highly developed areas like the south east of England.

Low-impact rural development

A stewardship economy provides new jobs in agriculture and horticulture and so encourages the repopulation of the countryside (Chapter 9). This in turn creates further work providing the services that these people need. The dilemma is that this will increase the amount of car use in the countryside, putting pressure not just on the road system but on greenhouse gas emissions. These will also increase because of the greater carbon emissions from space heating in isolated conventional homes. And there is a danger that poorly conceived new developments will blight the landscape.

These risks need to be counteracted by the planning system which should ensure that new developments are ecologically sound, carbon neutral, self-sufficient in energy and waste disposal as well as architecturally sympathetic. Some residents will want to build low impact homes that may not meet the planning requirements and building regulations but nevertheless need to be permitted.

Impact of planning decisions on stewardship fees

It is the whole community, not the individual landowner, that benefits in a stewardship economy when the market rent of land rises and loses when it falls. This is entirely appropriate because it is the community that creates these rises and falls in value. As the value of land depends on the use to which it can be put, planning restrictions reduce the stewardship fees of the land on which the restrictions are placed. On the other hand, if land previously designated as agricultural or parkland is subjected to a planning decision that allows it to be used for residential purposes, the stewardship fees rise. This increase in land value is automatically captured in a stewardship economy without any need for additional development charges or taxes (Stewardship Economy: Book 2)

Planning restrictions on one site also affect the value of other sites in the vicinity – for example, restricting a site to use as a park will usually increase the value of surrounding residential plots. However, the overall impact of the planning process on the total market rent of all the affected sites is unpredictable.

If the state imposes planning restrictions on a site the steward is automatically compensated by having to pay lower stewardship fees, while everyone shares the cost of the restrictions through the consequent reduction in our Universal Incomes.

27

Property developers play an important role in providing new buildings and other improvements. They should find it easier in a stewardship economy to acquire the land they need, as the existing stewards will be paying stewardship fees and will only hold on to land if they are making good use of it. If a developer has to pay stewardship fees for land that they are waiting to develop, this provides a strong incentive to progress the development.

Where a developer is building on a large site, they may have to put together the site by assembling several plots of land and a wide range of leaseholds and other interests, a process that can take years. They will have to apply for and gain planning permission and commission architects and builders to design and build the improvement. All of this requires substantial investment for a return that occurs only when the building has been completed and is either sold or rented. If the developer needs to pay stewardship fees while putting together a large and complicated site or going through a protracted planning process, the development might not be financially viable. This would be a particular problem if the stewardship fees were to rise as soon as planning permission is granted. To avoid this, it may be appropriate for planning authorities to grant planning permission that will take effect after a length of time that they judge to be realistic for completion of the development.

If the planning body were to be made responsible for paying the stewardship fees during the course of the planning application, it would have an incentive to reach decisions much more speedily. For this, it would need more generous funding.

Democratic planning

There is a risk of corruption in any planning process, and planning decisions have long-term financial consequences in a stewardship economy. Planning is both a technical and political process and must operate under democratic scrutiny. This is particularly important in a stewardship economy for two reasons: the need to prevent corruption, and the need to balance local and national consequences of planning decisions.

Stewardship requires a planning process that is clear, transparent, democratically accountable and impeccably carried out. Democratic planning in a stewardship economy requires the planning process to be well funded if local communities are to be in a sufficiently powerful position to influence the future of their area. The processes themselves need to build on existing asset-based and conversational approaches. One positive approach has been the development of approaches, such as 'Planning for real' http://www.planningforreal.org.uk/ that have arisen from the field of community development. These asset-based approaches, which recognise the strengths of existing communities, provide ways of mapping and putting to use these assets and of enabling local people to have productive conversations about the future that they would like to have for their area.

National planning priorities

In an ownership economy when national development priorities (for example, a new railway, power station, fracking site or nuclear waste dump) result in damage to a local area, residents and businesses may suffer a financial loss as the sale price of their home or premises falls and the environment deteriorates. In a stewardship economy the sale price of a building is unaffected and the stewardship fees fall, providing a subsidy for the loss of amenity that the development brings. The total sum available for distribution as Universal Income will be reduced by a small amount, and so it is the whole of society, rather than the individual steward, that bears the financial burden of necessary developments. For this proposal to work, valuations for stewardship fees must be readily adjusted downwards when market rents fall.

A stewardship economy can help with the situation where a site needs be selected for, for example, long-term storage of nuclear waste (within the country that has produced it). The first step would be at national level, to identify the safest and most desirable sites on geological grounds. Some of these then need to be ruled out, for example, because they are in areas of Special Scientific Interest or in National Parks. This would leave a shortlist of possible sites where local communities could be invited to bid for a subsidy for taking the facility. The community that is prepared to accept the lowest subsidy, which could be interpreted as the community that least objected to the facility, would receive the subsidy for accepting the waste storage. The subsidy could be paid out to the local population on an equal per capita basis or weighted towards those living closest to it or most likely to be affected by it. This is, in principle, similar to the payments currently paid to communities close to planned wind farms but in a stewardship economy the payment would be ongoing, rather than a one-off.

Where there are priorities for conservation purposes, in a stewardship economy the steward is likely to be happy to accept reasonable limitations on how they use the land, because their stewardship fees will decrease to compensate them for the reduced market rent of the site.

To summarise: A stewardship economy needs a strong, transparent and democratically accountable planning system that can counteract any excessive pressure to overdevelop. It must operate in a participative way so that its decisions truly reflect the common good, not commercial interests or the opinions of a distant bureaucracy.

In a stewardship economy there are no windfall financial gains to be had from relaxation of planning restrictions, and so no undue pressure by stewards for such relaxation. Provided that valuations are readily adjusted downwards when market rents fall, a stewardship economy automatically compensates stewards whose properties are adversely affected by planning decisions.

Stewardship places planning at the heart of the economy and enables it to determine land use rather than, at the most, permit it.

Chapter 3   Regions and cities

In ownership economies it is obvious that some regions are prosperous and have high levels of income, employment and land values while others are relatively deprived with poverty, unemployment, poor health and low land values. Younger people and those who are more highly trained tend to leave these areas of economic deprivation. And a downward spiral often takes hold in which enterprise is discouraged from locating or remaining in the area by the lack of skilled workers and poor infrastructure.

How would regions develop in a stewardship economy? Would there be regional disparities in economic activity and wealth just as there are in ownership economies? What would cities be like? Would they become more or less compact, would their land use and their occupants become more or less diverse?

Ownership economy

Geographical economics

Tony Vickers introduced the term 'landvaluescape' in 2000 to refer to the way in which the market value of land varies from place to place. These values can be represented on a 'value map', just as the height of land can be represented in a topographical map (Tony Vickers 2009: 14). He describes features of the landvaluescape that are recognisable by experts even without the need for computer visualisations – value peaks in city centres surrounded by troughs of inner city housing and industry; ridges along major roads; value troughs along the length of motorways and railways with peaks at intersections and stations; and scarp ridges next to water features.

This landvaluescape and associated value maps, particularly when overlaid on to topographical maps, provide a way of making sense of how geographic location impacts on the economy.

Regional development

The social problems of deprived areas in ownership economies are well rehearsed and include low income, unemployment, low educational achievement, poor health, social exclusion, crime, inability to obtain a mortgage and depopulation.

Prosperous areas have their problems too. High rents require businesses either to be highly profitable or to own their sites outright if they are to survive. And in these areas it is difficult to recruit workers in essential public services, particularly when their pay is negotiated nationally, and they are unable to afford local housing costs.

Land values are high in areas with a buoyant economy, a high rate of employment and high rates of pay. In an ownership economy, a house in a prosperous area might cost as much as 10–20 times more than an identical property in a less prosperous part of the same country.

Many countries, or free trade zones such as the European Union, try to reduce these inequalities by means of regeneration programmes that redistribute wealth from the prosperous to the poorer regions. These tend, however, to be short-term and so focus on investment in capital projects rather than long-term support.

Cities

Cities are responsible for a large proportion of global economic output and their importance is growing as the knowledge economy reinforces the importance of business clusters. However, the high price of land in cities squeezes out important sorts of land use that fail to generate enough profit. The land market does not, on its own, provide the necessary parks, public spaces or public services or even commercial, industrial and agricultural activities in close proximity to residential areas.

Parks and public spaces

A park is rarely the most economically productive use of a particular site. In ownership economies parks have often been set aside as public goods by a private owner, charitable body or local government. They remain free from development either because of the terms of the original bequest or because of planning restrictions.

Some advocate introducing charges for admission, so that users of the park provide an income stream for its owners. But this revenue is still likely to be less than could be achieved by building on it and charges discourage people from using the park, which makes it less valuable to society. Planning restrictions remain the most effective mechanism for promoting and preserving parks, provided that the planning authorities are truly independent of commercial pressure.

Diversity

Jane Jacobs (1961) championed the importance of diversity in a well-functioning city. She recognised the advantages of mixed communities where there are 'eyes on the street' at all times of day, which limit antisocial behaviour and promote community cohesion. These include parents and children going to and from school, workers going to lunch in the cafés and returning for a drink after work, and people going to restaurants in the evenings.

These communities contrast with homogenous developments that are deserted for long periods of time – suburbs empty by day, commercial districts empty outside office hours – and residential areas that are generally segregated by housing tenure, wealth, class and race. The planning system has tended to favour developments that separate residential from industrial and even from commercial uses, as a reaction against the polluted living conditions in Victorian industrial cities. However, the need to separate residential development from industrial and commercial is much less of an issue with modern industries. And the environmental and social benefits of reducing commuting by enabling people to work close to their homes are compelling.

A lack of 'eyes on the street' results partly from the homogenous developments but also from the significant amount of land in cities that is unused, unoccupied homes, empty offices or shops, derelict buildings and land.

While homogenous development may lead to the maximum economic use of land in an ownership economy, the uneconomic use of land can support the diversity of the people who live and work there. Cities include areas of deprivation, which of course has negative impacts like crime and the fear of crime. But these areas also provide areas where people on low incomes can live, and businesses of low profitability can survive. The availability of low-value land close to areas of prosperity enables cities to be dynamic and diverse places in which start-up businesses and artists can establish themselves in localities that have fallen out of fashion and out of use. Even in areas of gentrification where market rents have risen, some owner-occupiers or protected tenants remain. Some shops that reflect the enthusiasms of their owners and might not be very profitable are able to continue in business because their premises are owned outright (or are at least held on a long lease) and do not need to pay a commercial rent.

Stewardship economy

Greater geographical equality

In a stewardship economy the same level of Universal Income is paid across the whole country, while stewardship fees are high in areas that are prosperous and low in areas that are poor. In this way, stewardship provides a mechanism that continuously and automatically redistributes the market rent of land from areas where per capita land values are high to areas where they are low. This reduces inequalities between individuals, neighbourhoods and regions. Stewardship reduces geographical inequality both at the level of the city and of the region.

Regional development

This transfer of resources through Universal Income and lower stewardship fees benefits local people and local businesses in poorer areas, stimulating enterprise and development where it is needed. The increased income puts money into the local economy, enables people to start their own business or take on part-time work. It provides some resources which, alongside regional banks that invest locally, could provide capital for local businesses. Private sector firms have an incentive to re-locate and invest capital in the marginal land in more deprived areas where stewardship fees, and so business costs, are low. In this way economic development – and, so, demand for housing – is distributed much more evenly around the country in a stewardship economy. This happens automatically, without the need for regeneration funding. During transition to a stewardship economy there would still be a need for institutional structures to support regeneration.

The increased economic activity leads to a virtuous cycle of rising land values, and so of rising stewardship fees, in previously poor areas. This provides a mechanism for funding other public goods such as public transport, schools. (Chapter 19).

Cities

Parks, public spaces and food production

If there were no planning restrictions in place, an urban park would be developed for some other use in a stewardship economy just as it would in an ownership economy. Indeed, the pressure to develop the land would be even greater in a stewardship economy because the steward of the site must pay fees equal to the market rent. The only effective counterbalance to this is the planning system which disallows certain uses. Where planning restrictions are imposed, the market rent of the site – and, so, the stewardship fees – will be lower. So, if planning regulations require the land to be used as a park with a universal right of access and maintained to a high standard, its stewardship fees would be low and might be negative. The revenue from stewardship fees lost by maintaining land as a park will be at least partially counterbalanced by an increase in stewardship fees from the sites close by, whose residents pay a premium for the views and easy access.

Sustainable cities need to contribute to their own food production and provide green space to mitigate flash flooding. A planning system should set aside urban land for horticulture and city farms as well as parks.

Collective action through the planning process in a stewardship economy is quite capable of providing for public goods and the central place of planning means that more thought is likely to be given to such matters than is usual in an ownership economy.

Diversity

More land is in use in a stewardship economy, leading to lower market rents than in an equivalent ownership economy and to greater affordability. However, underused land attracts stewardship fees equal to the full market rent of the site, so relatively unprofitable businesses and low-rent housing would be under some financial pressure to relocate to an area with lower market rents. There is, therefore, a danger that stewardship might lead to more homogenous occupancy. If cities lack a sufficient mix of use, age and social class in a stewardship economy, it might be necessary to take steps to increase diversity, for example, by imposing planning restrictions that designate some properties for particular uses and so hold market rents down, or even by direct subsidies. The aim would be to support mixed neighbourhoods, not to recreate large housing developments with a single form of housing tenure.

Stewardship also influences the patterns of transport in a city. Commuting is less attractive as people pay the true cost price of fuel, and less necessary as land is put to better use. Inner city development is more mixed, with residential land and light industry balancing the commercial.

Chapter 4   Housing

The lack of decent housing that everyone can afford in the UK at present is caused by many factors, and, of course, there is no single or simple solution. On the supply side these factors include the rate of supply of new truly affordable housing and the number of existing homes that are empty or underused, which pushes up market rents and market values. On the demand side, low rates of pay and unemployment make housing unaffordable and the rising number of households requiring accommodation push up market rents and market values.

The most important set of factors that make housing unaffordable, however, are a set of deliberate government policies. One set includes restricting supply - of council housing and housing association homes that can be afforded on local wages. Another set of polices boosts demand, by removing caps on mortgage loan-to-value, help-to-buy schemes and through the structure of the tax system.

All of these factors need to be tackled. Political choices will be as important and as varied in a stewardship economy as in an ownership economy. The focus of this book, however, is primarily on the impact that replacing ownership by stewardship of land and replacing orthodox taxes and subsidies with stewardship fees. Once the transition to stewardship has begun, many of the other necessary policies will be easier to envisage and enact.

Ownership economy

Decent housing that everyone can afford?

Many people find it difficult to find a decent home that they can afford. Young adults in work may have to live with their parents because they can't afford their own home. Workers may have to commute long distances with the associated costs to themselves of time, money and stress, and costs to society in the form of congestion, climate change and loss of social cohesion.

In the UK in 2006, the average price of a home in 65 per cent of towns and cities was not affordable by key workers such as teachers, police, ambulance workers and nurses(Guardian 29/7/2006). People in this 'intermediate market' are too poor to buy, but not poor enough to meet the criteria for renting from a social landlord that provides subsidised housing. In London, these workers can't afford the market rent or mortgage payments even for a one-bedroom flat, and generally have to leave London when they want to start a family. The problem is even greater in rural areas, where agricultural workers and other local people are driven out of their native villages by commuters or retirees. Rural homeowners need to spend 52 per cent of their net income on housing compared with 32 per cent in cities.

This is a tragedy for individuals and communities. The Joseph Rowntree Foundation (2001 Land Inquiry) found that a lack of affordable housing is threatening the viability of both urban and rural areas, and that it creates inflexibilities in the labour market that threaten the UK's international competitiveness.

Rising house prices

A house is, or can be, both a home and an investment. It is this dual nature, and the tensions between the two, that make housing such an emotive and complicated issue.

A house as a home

Most people have times in their life – as students, during training, early years in their career – when they need to be able to move from place to place every few years. But most people also experience long periods when they want to put down roots in a particular place because they are settled in their job, because they have children who will benefit from growing up with a group of peers at school, or because they want to cultivate a particular piece of land. At these times it's also a great advantage to be able to modify the structure of their home – to re-decorate, insulate, add a bedroom or a mobility ramp – without being subject to the whims of a landlord. Being an owner-occupier provides freedom and security.

Renting, rather than buying a car is becoming an increasingly popular option. It can be more convenient and transfers more of the responsibility to the manufacturer for maintenance and recycling.

There may be similar arguments in favour of renting a home, particularly in countries where regulation provides for greater tenants' rights, longer tenancies and rent controls. But in the UK, where regulation favours the landlords, owner-occupation is an attractive option.

One of the benefits of owner-occupation is the way that housing costs are experienced across a lifecycle. Owner-occupiers make mortgage payments while they have a mortgage and the interest payments that they make are very broadly comparable to the payments that tenants make for rent, sometimes more, sometimes less depending on whether they have a repayment mortgage or an interest-only mortgage with some other mechanism for paying off the amount borrowed. Once the mortgage has been paid off they can live rent-free for the rest of their life, through the years of retirement when their earnings are likely to be at their lowest. In the UK this is the major provision that most owner-occupiers make for their financial independence in retirement. These lifecycle benefits are not dependent on any increase in house prices.

A house as an investment

The other reason for owning a house is as an investment – most clearly when it is let out to tenants, but even an owner-occupied house serves this function. Indeed, in times of rapid house price growth the increase in wealth to be had from owning your own home may be greater than your income from work. People may take on as expensive a house as they can afford, even if it is larger than they actually need.

It's not surprising that we are pleased by every announcement that house prices have risen. There is something magical about the effortless and seemingly inexorable rise in the value of our homes throughout much of the economic cycle, and we forget the times when prices stagnate or fall. Most of our other possessions decline in value and eventually need to be replaced. But our houses can rise in value while we sit on the sofa, dreaming of making a small fortune by buying more property and letting it to students or enjoying a holiday house abroad. No wonder there have been so many TV programmes about doing up houses – we can imagine making as much money by buying just the right property in the right place at the right time as we do from a lifetime of work.

When share values rise this is, at least in theory, because they represent a share in the growth of real productive assets. When house prices rise, it is not (usually) because the buildings have become bigger or better. The rise in house prices is predominantly a rise in the value of the land on which they are built. In the USA land accounts for a third of the cost of housing, and a half in cities. Building costs, adjusted for inflation, have not risen for 30 years (Economist 24/4/14: 19). One of the few jurisdictions to value land and buildings separately on a plot-by-plot basis is the Canadian province of British Columbia. Over the 20 years to 1999, the value of buildings rose by 247 per cent while the value of the land increased by 652 per cent (Fred Harrison 2005:175). This long-term appreciation in the value of land makes home ownership a much more attractive investment than renting for those who are able to do so, at most stages of the economic cycle.

Do owner-occupiers benefit from rising house prices?

While we all need somewhere to live so if the price of our house doubles there is no direct benefit to be had until we die, and our relatives receive a share of the sale price. There are, however, strategies for benefiting indirectly from rising house prices: downsizing, equity release and borrowing. An owner can downsize by moving to a smaller home, or a home in a less desirable area, for example, when children leave home. If they sell the home at the time when they are no longer able to live independently, this can provide funding for residential or nursing care in old age. 'Equity release' schemes allow an owner-occupier to sell a proportion of the rights to the house to an investment company while they remain in residence until they choose to sell the property. Or the owner can use their home as security to borrow money at a more favourable rate than on an unsecured loan. The home, here, is not really a source of wealth; it is simply security for increasing levels of debt. Owner-occupiers have the great advantage of being able to live rent-free once they have paid off their mortgage, but rising house prices provide advantages that are mainly illusory.

Risks of ownership

The risks of rising house prices are often forgotten, particularly during the years before a property bubble bursts. People who buy near the peak of a boom may find that they develop negative equity –

that their debt exceeds the market value of their house. They may be able to ride this out for a few years until house prices rise again but there are big risks for those who have to move, whether this is to find work or for family reasons, and for those who lose their jobs and can't keep up the regular mortgage payments. They find themselves in a financial trap not because they have chosen to speculate in the housing market, but simply because they wanted a home. Homes are particularly likely to be re-possessed when the collapse of a house price bubble is accompanied, as it often is, by high interest rates or unemployment.

In the UK more than 1 million people were left in negative equity after the 1989 property crash, when house prices fell by about 30 per cent and took until 1995 to return to 1989 values. In Tokyo in the 1990s, with its 100-year mortgages, house prices fell by more than 50 per cent and remained stagnant for more than a decade.

House prices are vulnerable to local factors as well as to the national economy. Development on a neighbouring site that blocks the view; poor maintenance of neighbouring properties; a local source of noise or pollution; new evidence of flood risk, site contamination or subsidence; even positive developments such as a residential unit for people with learning difficulties may cause a fall in nearby property prices. The loss of value may be even more extreme – for example when there is radioactive contamination that requires long-term evacuation of properties, such as occurred around Fukushima in 2011.

Damage caused by rising house prices

Rising house prices reflect a buoyant economy and stimulate that economy by making homeowners feel more wealthy and stimulating spending. So, it is not surprising that house price rises are encouraged by government and celebrated in the press. But what a crazy situation this is. If any other consumer goods were to rise in price, we would decry this example of inflation eroding our living standards. Rising house prices means that people need to take on more debt to buy their home, and many young people have been priced out of the housing market altogether.

Rising house prices amplify the benefits of living rent-free that exist even when house prices are stable. While tenants pay market rents that rise over the years, the mortgage payments made by owner-occupiers reflect the historic value of the property at the time they bought it, not its current value.

But there are risks to the individual homeowner, particularly from the debt that they take on and even when house prices rise the benefits are not as real as they seem. House price rises creates inequalities between homeowners and tenants and between the generations and they lead to underinvestment in productive enterprise. Pushing house prices ever higher is an easy way for a government to please a substantial part of their constituency and to stimulate the economy in the short term, even if this means risking cycles of boom and bust.

It has been suggested that high and rising land values are necessary for developers, who do indeed benefit if land values rise during the building project just as they lose if land values fall. But to build, rather than profit from speculation, builders only need to be sure that land prices will not fall and that there will be a demand for their completed product. Over an economic cycle, fluctuation in land prices are damaging to builders, as can be seen from their struggle in the aftermath of the credit crunch of 2007 and subsequent banking collapse. High land values in themselves increase developers' costs and reduce their profits as a proportion of costs.

Rising house prices are a problem that is highly visible to all those who aspire to own a home, a group that now includes the majority of younger people.

Government policy and land values

Although there has probably never been a time when London has had an adequate supply of houses that people can afford, the severity of current problems in London and across the country can be traced almost entirely to government policy. This has consistently boosted land values, whether intentionally or inadvertently.

One telling clue, however, is that governments have introduced an economic stimulus whenever there is a risk of house prices falling. This was particularly evident with the introduction of quantitative easing in 2008, intended both to protect the banks and to shore up house prices by reducing interest rates on mortgages. There are examples from the post-war Labour administration (1945-51), the subsequent years of Conservative government (1951-64), the Wilson, Heath Callaghan years (1964-79) with the Development Levy

(Wilson 1967), Development Gains Tax (Heath 1973/4), Development Land Tax (Callaghan 1976).

The Thatcher government (1979-90) brought in a raft of policies that changed forever the housing market in the UK. Some of these had their main impact on the rental market, where subsidised rental tenants (social tenants) were incentivised to move out of council housing or housing association accommodation into private rented housing. This left the country with inadequate amounts of social housing and a great deal of private rental housing that is substandard and insecure, while the payment of Housing Benefit enriches landlords, drains government resources and inflates house prices.

Other policies had their main impact on the market value of homes, in particular the abolition of the domestic rates (better remembered as the introduction of the Poll Tax) and the financial deregulation that introduced competition into the mortgage market and made loans available at much higher loan-to-value ratios. In 1988 Thatcher took the courageous step of announcing that Mortgage Interest Relief at Source (MIRAS) would be restricted, in particular so that it would apply to only one person per property. Backdating the change from March to August fuelled a frenzy of speculative buying by couples, pushing house prices to a peak.

The political unpopularity of the Poll Tax (Community Charge) was a key factor in Thatcher's downfall, and John Major's government set about replacing it by the council tax (1993). Disguised as a property tax and incorporating a 'drive-by' valuation carried out in 1991, this is more like a Poll Tax than a tax based on property values. Council tax is particularly regressive, falling up to fifteen times more heavily on low value homes than on high value homes and paid by the occupier, that is to say in many cases by the tenant. Another aspect of the regressive nature of council tax is that it reduces the market value of low-value homes while it increases the market value of high-value homes.

Exemption of owner-occupiers from Capital Gains Tax increases the value of the investment in a home, which in turn leads to increased demand for homes and higher prices.

Stamp Duty, a transaction tax, discourages or prevents the transfer of homes.

Stewardship economy

A stewardship economy is far more stable than in an ownership economy. Stewardship fees rise and fall with the economy in a way that is countercyclical. When the economy is booming stewardship fees rise, slowing down growth and the potential for inflation; when growth is negative they fall, reducing the financial burden on the steward and providing a financial stimulus.

This section describes a steady-state stewardship economy. The principles of transition, which needs to start from where we are and respect existing property rights, is set out in book 2 as are the practical details, starting with a reform of the council tax

Adequate income

A stewardship economy provides several mechanisms that increase the income of people in lower-paid jobs: Universal Income; increased levels of pay; removal of National Insurance Contributions and Income Tax.

Universal Income funded from stewardship fees redistributes wealth from those using more than their fair share of the land to those using less than their fair share. A fair share of the land does not mean an equal area for all, but an area of equal market rent. Poorer people find that this makes their housing, which is usually in locations that are of less than average desirability, more affordable than in an ownership economy. But a Universal Income will not make housing affordable for poor families in affluent parts of cities. If we are to achieve diverse communities, rates of pay should reflect the local level of stewardship fees. In the public sector, pay in a stewardship economy should include an element that reflects the level of stewardship fees for a home in the area in which they work, rather like the London weighting. In the private sector this would result in higher costs to consumers or firms would have to move to areas where stewardship fees are lower.

House as home or investment

In a stewardship economy there may be good reasons to choose to be a steward-occupier rather than to rent. These advantages include greater security; no need to deal with a landlord and freedom to modify the property. But people can choose whether to steward or to rent without the possibility of making a financial gain affecting their decision.

In an established stewardship economy, the purchase price of land is zero. This does not mean that the cost of occupying the land is low but that, rather than paying the market value of the land up front as in an ownership economy, the steward pays its market rent while they occupy it, as stewardship fees. Everyone benefits, by receiving an equal Universal Income from the market rent of all land and this income enables them to pay rent for the land of which they are tenant or steward.

Even during a transition period to a stewardship economy (book 2) there is an immediate a cap on the market value of land. These stewardship fees do not directly reduce land values, as they would if a Land Value Tax was imposed that is proportional to land values, but the transition mechanism guarantees that land values will not rise.

A steward owns the building, the depreciated replacement cost of which changes little through the economic cycle, so nobody finds themselves plunged into negative equity. If a local development makes a home less desirable the steward loses none of their investment when they come to sell and, in the meanwhile, is compensated by paying lower stewardship fees. In addition, stewardship eliminates the transfer of wealth from tenants to landlords and owner-occupiers and from future generations to present homeowners.

In a stewardship economy there is a greater supply of homes and housing land because there are financial incentives to dispose of an under-used asset such as an empty or second home and to develop brownfield sites.

There is also less demand for homes to purchase because owning a home and being its steward has no financial advantage over renting. There are no capital gains to be had from the rising value of land and no speculative tinge to house prices. The financial incentives of stewardship fees and Universal Income may combine to encourage people to live in shared households rather than alone.

These supply and demand factors reduce the market rent of housing land and so make it more affordable. In addition, wealth is transferred from people occupying sites that are more desirable than average to people occupying sites that are less desirable than average through the combination of stewardship fees and Universal Income.

In spite of all these factors, however, a stewardship economy may, particularly during transition, need to use additional mechanisms to ensure that people can afford a home. Such mechanism include the planning system, Community Land Trusts, subsidised rental housing and Housing Benefit.

Chapter 5 Countryside

A stewardship economy is rooted in the understanding that we who are alive today are not owners of this planet but its stewards, and so have a responsibility for the long-term future of the planet and the wellbeing of future generations. A stewardship economy would be more open than an ownership economy to measures that protect the environment. In a stewardship economy we would probably be more ready than we are now to take early action when some threat to the environment is recognised. And we would have a powerful practical tool to tackle environmental protection – a way of thinking about and handling property rights in the natural world.

The way that people live in and use the countryside depends on the property system that is in place. How would farming be different in a stewardship economy? Would there be more people living on the land or fewer, what would be the size of landholdings, what agricultural practices would people follow and what would the mix of farming be? What are the implications of stewardship for rural transport and rural life more generally?

Ownership economy

Agriculture

Economic factors shape, or even determine, many aspects of agriculture such as agricultural practices, employment opportunities and the price of food.

Economics

Agriculture is one of the few industries, along with banking and nuclear power, to which governments in ownership economies provide large subsidies over an indefinite timescale. Government support for agriculture is intended to benefit farmers, support poor rural communities, ensure food security and support conservation of the environment. Direct subsidies to UK farmers are officially around £3 billion a year, although Kevin Cahill (2002:402) suggested that official figures underestimate the real total by well over £1bn.

Subsidies can take the form of:

- intervention purchases to support (increase) the market price of agricultural produce
- production subsidies
- production quotas
- set-aside payments
- extensification payments to reduce the number of livestock
- subsidies that promote carbon-intensive farming such as cheap diesel fuel and fertiliser subsidies
- payments under the Defra Environmental Stewardship agreements, introduced in 2005 to:
  o conserve wildlife (biodiversity, including genetic conservation)
  o maintain and enhance landscape quality and character
  o protect the historic environment and natural resources
  o promote public access and understanding of the countryside
  o protect natural resources
  o manage flood risk.

There are also tax reductions and exemptions on:

- Uniform Business Rate (most farmland and farm buildings)
- Inheritance Tax on family farms
- Capital Gains Tax (rollover relief).

We have paid for these subsidies as taxpayers and as consumers. The Common Agricultural Policy of the European Union cost EU taxpayers around £34 billion per year in direct payments. And as consumers we have all paid food prices that are inflated by many of these policies.

Duncan Pickard, a farmer, retired academic and advocate of Land Value Taxation, has described the negative impact of taxes on employment in agriculture (Duncan Pickard 2004:43) and a whole range of distortions and unexpected knock-on consequences from agricultural subsidies. Intervention purchases have increased the price of food for consumers and created food mountains and lakes. Inheritance Tax exemption increases demand for agricultural land as a means of tax avoidance. Payments for set-aside and extensification increase the demand for agricultural land that is left idle. Farms are encouraged to maximise the amount of land they own, leading to large farms swallowing small farms (funded by the subsidies themselves). The acquisition of outlying fields leads to inefficiencies and poor husbandry (Duncan Pickard 2004:43). Subsidised diesel fuel increases the mechanisation of farming and reduces employment in agriculture.

Subsidies do not benefit tenant farmers, other than in the very short term because any improvement in profitability increases the market rent of the land, which translates into an increase in the rent they have to pay.

In addition, subsidies distort international trade, particularly in their impact on low-consumption economies. Tariffs and subsidies by high-consumption economies have been a major reason why successive rounds of talks (Doha and Uruguay) have been abandoned at the World Trade Organisation.

Market value of agricultural land

Farm owners do benefit as the value of their land rises. When local authority rates were removed from agricultural land in 1929 the rents paid by tenant farmers rose, and as a result so did the market value of agricultural land; food prices did not fall. The currently high market value of agricultural land is actively harmful to the business of farming in two major ways. The cost deters new entrants to farming and any farmer with a mortgage is paying interest costs that often make the business unprofitable.

Land can be an attractive investment vehicle even for those with no interest in farming, particularly to offset capital gains made elsewhere and to optimise estate planning. This has led to land being acquired by absentee landlords and institutional investors. Land ownership is consolidated in the hands of smaller numbers of investors as the revenue from subsidies is reinvested in buying neighbouring land.

In ownership economies the financial burden of society's aspirations for conservation falls on the landowner, who may be tempted to oppose or ignore the requirements.

Agricultural practice

Providing information about 'food miles' is an attempt to help consumers understand the true costs of their food (true cost pricing), but it is limited because it focuses on just one sort of environmental damage caused by food production. Although we currently give most attention to carbon dioxide, other greenhouse gases need to be considered. These include methane, which has 23 times more impact on the climate than carbon dioxide. The main source of methane is agriculture, particularly livestock, and true cost pricing to include the cost of methane emissions permit would increase the cost of animal produce. There are a range of other costs that farmers do not currently have to take into account, for example, the cost of dealing with the copper that contaminates pig slurry or the nitrates that cause eutrophication of watercourses such as the Norfolk and Suffolk broads.

Colin Tudge (2003:47) identifies a range of requirements for farming: that it produces food of sufficient quality, nutritional value, appeal and safety in a way that is sustainable, considerate to domestic animals and wildlife-friendly and provides employment and justice for those who work the land. He refers to this constellation of attributes that conforms to ecological and ethical imperatives as 'enlightened husbandry'.

Farmers have to maximise their output per pound invested if they are to operate profitably. In an era of cheap oil and water this has meant using large inputs of agricultural machinery, chemicals and water. Agriculture has been transformed as pesticides and new seed varieties have permitted monocultures, herbicides have reduced the need for crop rotation and fertilisers have reduced the need for fallow and animal manure.

If you take account of land used for feedstock production, the livestock sector is responsible for 70 per cent of agricultural land use and 18 per cent of total greenhouse gas emissions– more than the transport sector. The increased consumption of meat in India and China is an important factor in their increased output of greenhouse gases. Demand for biofuels is already causing an increased demand for land, rainforest destruction and a reduction of land available for food crops.

Changes in agricultural practice, combined with taxes on labour like National Insurance Contributions and Income Tax as well as fuel subsidies for agriculture, have reduced the need for agricultural labour. Only 2 per cent of the workforce in the UK is currently employed on the land. At the same time Regional Development Agencies and regeneration programmes view job creation as one of the main measures of success. Many people would like to find work and accommodation in the countryside and working on the land can improve health and wellbeing.

Food prices are already rising due to many factors including demand from the increasingly wealthy middle classes in low-consumption economies, the rising cost of oil-based agricultural inputs and pressure on land from the cultivation of biofuels – and at times speculation. Enlightened husbandry, and particularly the provision of humane conditions for livestock, further increases the cost of food in the short term.

Compaction by heavy machinery on farms and lack of manure have led to a reduction in soil quality. Economic factors have led to consolidation of landholdings, and the mechanisation of agriculture made possible by fossil fuel inputs also contributed to hedgerow destruction. In combination with the heavy use of pesticides this has led to wildlife destruction. And the lack of skilled agricultural labour has led to poor maintenance of hedges and ditches.

Rural transport and services

People living in the countryside have further to travel to work, shops and entertainment than people living in cities. There is inevitably less access to public transport and there will always be a greater reliance on personal transport, particularly cars. Private and public transport, like postal services and utilities, cost more to provide in rural areas. For these reasons, increases in the costs of fuel and driving are felt more heavily but have less impact on driving behaviour than in urban areas. True cost pricing, with fuel costs that reflect the cost of climate change, tend to be strongly opposed by people living in the countryside.

While there may be a very good case for new residential development in the countryside, the risk is that, like existing rural communities, people moving there will require greater expenditure of carbon on heating and transport than urban dwellers.

Stewardship economy

Agriculture

Economics

Agriculture accounts for the use of about 75 per cent of the land in the UK and forestry accounts for another 10 per cent. When people first hear of proposals for a stewardship economy, they may imagine that 85 per cent stewardship fees would fall on agriculture and forestry. But stewardship fees are equal to the market rent of land, which is hundreds or even thousands of times higher per hectare in the city than in the countryside. In a stewardship economy only 7 per cent of all stewardship fees in the UK would fall on agricultural and forestry land.

Another fear is that farmers would be driven off marginal land by the stewardship fees that they would have to pay. But hill farmers make very efficient use of the land at their disposal and when this sort of land is transferred in the market bidders are unlikely to offer an excessively high market rent. Where land truly is marginal and it is not possible to make any income by using it, its market rent is zero or negative and, as discussed below, stewardship would provide an automatic subsidy at a level determined by the market. If, on the other hand, there is competition from other commercial users, as in an ownership economy, we need a functioning planning system to retain it in agricultural use where this is in the public interest.

Agriculture has no tax advantage over other businesses in a stewardship economy. Like all other stewards of land, they pay stewardship fees and environmental charges and are exempt from all other taxes and charges. As farmers in the UK at present receive a variety of incentives which would no longer apply, they would not benefit as much as other businesses in the transition to a stewardship economy. They would also be liable for the true cost pricing of greenhouse gas emissions and water and there would be a different approach to subsidies.

The impact on farming of a stewardship economy will depend on whether the farmer had previously been a tenant farmer or landowner. A tenant farmer finds their position essentially unchanged; they continue to make the same regular payment to their landlord, comprising rent for the land and rental for the

52

improvements (buildings). An agricultural (absentee) landlord in a stewardship economy still owns their buildings and improvements and receives any rental payments for these but they pay stewardship fees equal to the market rent of the land. This means that the land itself has zero market value (sale price) as it no longer generates any income net of fees. There is less incentive to be an agricultural landlord in a stewardship economy as the yield on improvements is not high. A more likely scenario is that of an owner-occupier farmer. They pay stewardship fees (market rent) to the Land Stewardship Trust, and any mortgage is needed only to buy the improvements on the land, not the land itself.

Of course, this description is not a practical approach to transition to a stewardship economy as it unfairly confiscates the market value of the land from the current owner.

The planning system prescribes or proscribes how land is to be used. The requirements it imposes on farmers in a stewardship economy would probably be very similar to those developed by the British government for farmers to receive payments under the Defra Environmental Stewardship agreements (Defra 2007). Success in meeting these requirements would be monitored in the same way in a stewardship economy as in the Defra Environmental Stewardship agreements.

Stewardship tends to bring underused land into cultivation because there are no incentives to keep land idle. However, pressure to bring land, particularly marginal land, into production could be destructive to the environment so this would need to be carefully monitored and, where necessary, prevented though the planning mechanism. Stewardship can promote appropriate conservation and improvement of the landscape through the planning system by designating unsightly and inappropriate developments as disimprovements. There is then a financial incentive on the steward to remove them, and not to build them in the first place. The planning system is also essential to preserve areas for wildlife and wilderness.

Husbandry clauses (Jonty Williams 2014: 24), describing the responsibilities of the steward to the land, are an integral part of stewardship and embody the planning requirements desired by the community.

The amount of any 'subsidy' for meeting the planning requirements would be decided not by government, or by the Land Stewardship

Trust, but by market mechanisms. When agricultural land is transferred to a new steward the bids that are made to secure its stewardship reflect its profitability, and this in turn depends on the planning requirements to which it is subject. Bids for stewardship fees will be lower where there are onerous planning requirements, thereby subsidising the farmer to meet them. Bidders can even offer a negative bid in that they can offer to accept responsibility for this land in exchange for the payments of a negative stewardship fee. This provides an automatic subsidy. Farmers would not be burdened by the bureaucracy of subsidies, or that of taxes such as VAT, Income Tax and National Insurance Contributions.

In a stewardship economy the market value of agricultural land is zero and there is no expectation that this will rise over time. There would be few institutional investors or other large landowners, and no one invests in farmland to escape taxes. The costs of stewarding underused land, including inefficiently used land at a distance from the main holding, would be greater. Less land is held by absentee landlords, and more by steward-occupiers. Farms are more compact and smaller. There is more opportunity for new entrants to farming because there is no need to borrow large sums of money to buy a farm. Farmland comes onto the market more frequently as it is not held in large parcels as a long-term investment.

In a stewardship economy, regulations that promote conservation reduce the market rent of land and so reduce the stewardship fees. Landlords are compensated for the requirements of society, and everyone bears the cost as they receive (slightly) lower levels of Universal Income.

The agricultural workforce is likely to be higher in a stewardship economy for several reasons. Stewardship fees provide an incentive to maximise production per hectare rather than per pound invested. Absence of taxes on employment and availability the Universal Income make workers more affordable; without the need to pay National Insurance Contributions and Income Tax for their workers, farmers could employ 50 per cent more people. The higher cost of fuel, fertiliser and labour-saving machinery encourages more labour-intensive practices.

This increase in the agricultural workforce makes for a more vibrant rural community. It reduces the isolation of farmers, described by Duncan Pickard (2004:22) and related by him to the high levels of suicide in the industry. It allows farmers to engage in more complex husbandry than the familiar monocultures that can be managed with a smaller workforce. And it allows them to give more attention to the detail of cultivation and more care and kindness to livestock.

Agricultural practice

Stewardship shifts the balance of agriculture between pastoral (grazing), arable (growing crops by the field) and horticulture (tending crops plant-by-plant). The increase in workforce makes it possible to devote more time, effort and land to horticulture, which is capable of high levels of output per acre. Meat and dairy are a much more carbon-intensive source of calories than plants and this would be reflected in higher true cost pricing, leading to a reduction in demand. Other environmental costs of pastoralism, such as soil erosion, water use, ammonia production and water pollution will, when incorporated into a true cost price for meat and dairy produce, further depress demand. On the other hand, a small amount of livestock will play its part in the mixed farm where it is valued for its manure (as the prices of chemical inputs rise) and ability to make use of marginal land and agricultural waste. Small farms may be less likely to invest in specialist processing machinery and so more likely to diversify their crops, reducing the risk of pests and infections. Reduced use of machinery, pesticides, and greater input of labour, lead to more variety and, it is to be hoped, more careful attention to soil quality and boundary hedges. Colin Tudge describes this rebalancing as the foundation for an enlightened husbandry (Colin Tudge 2003:357) that conforms to ecological and ethical imperatives. The landscape in a stewardship economy is more diverse and supports greater biodiversity as well as more people living on the land.

There has been considerable debate about the yields per acre of organic farming compared with traditional farming. Peter Melchett (2007) claims that, if all agriculture was organic, small reductions in yields in the northern hemisphere would be more than offset by gains elsewhere. The gains from organic agriculture are particularly significant in drought conditions, which will surely become more frequent in many areas. In a stewardship economy soil quality is assessed and, where it has become eroded or degraded, the steward is required to pay the disimprovement value. Farmers would no longer have a financial incentive to exhaust the soil. Higher oil prices in a stewardship economy favour organic farming, with inorganic fertilisers replaced by crop rotation and the greater use of compost and manure.

The conduct of agriculture, perhaps more than any other business, depends critically on whether costs and benefits are internalised or externalised and on the discount factor that is applied to determine the time frame that farmers take into consideration. Most businesses can discount the future at more than 1 per cent and so ignore the future beyond the next 30-100 years, while agriculture in its ecological context has a time horizon of something more like 10,000 years. The sustainability of agriculture is a matter of human survival. Stewardship promotes sustainability by ensuring that agriculture does not externalise its costs and by providing a context in which the future is not discounted or discounted very little.

Increased transport costs in a stewardship economy (through true cost pricing for fuel) generally favour domestic production of food. This may reduce demand for land in countries that currently export food and increase demand in countries that currently import. However, the production of New Zealand lamb for consumption in the UK is less energy-intensive than the production of British lamb, for example, and the energy cost of transporting food such as tomatoes may not be as much as growing the same crops in heated greenhouses in the UK. In general, communities and countries are likely to produce more of their own basic foodstuffs and so be more able to cope in a crisis where external sources of food are unavailable or unaffordable.

True cost prices paid by farmers for energy, water, fertilisers and any environmental damage will feed through into higher food prices in a stewardship economy. The price increases will particularly affect out-of-season food, imports and energy-intensive foods like meat. True cost pricing of food would lead to increased consumption of fruit and vegetables and reduce meat and dairy, in line with our understanding of what constitutes a healthy diet and the imperatives of enlightened husbandry.

Rural transport and services

Increasing the costs of necessary road travel in the countryside (by true cost pricing of fuel) causes a fall in the market rent of rural land. These reduced stewardship fees provide automatic compensation for people living in the countryside. This means that people living in the country are not, on average, penalised by the costs of fuel but each individual still has an incentive to reduce their consumption of petrol.

This provides an example of the way in which environmental charges (in this case, true cost pricing for petrol) would have a different impact around the country when applied in a stewardship economy rather than in our current economy. It also illustrates how environmental charges do not generate additional net revenue in a stewardship economy as the revenue they do generate is offset by a fall in stewardship fees. In a similar way, it would be possible to allow postal services and utilities to charge the true costs of providing these services in rural areas because price increases lead to compensatory falls in the market rent and so in the stewardship fees of affected properties.

A growing agricultural workforce in a stewardship economy will need housing developments which must be ecologically sound, carbon neutral and self-sufficient in energy and waste disposal and this will require strong planning requirements. These should include the provision for public transport and measures to discourage commuting by car into urban centres.

In summary: In a stewardship economy we would find smaller mixed farms with more people with their own landholdings and more people working more intensively on more land – but in more varied ways. Stewards make no initial outlay to purchase land, paying only for the buildings and other improvements. They pay stewardship fees for land used, except on marginal land where fees would be zero, or even negative, providing a subsidy for caring for the land. Food production will be more local and organic and food prices higher, particularly energy-intensive foods like meat and dairy.

Wealthy people would disinvest from agricultural property as it no longer allows them to avoid tax, and people who want to use the land productively will move in. Any new developments of rural housing would need to be subject to planning requirements to ensure that they do not increase road transport.

Part II The environment and climate

A stewardship economy is rooted in the understanding that we who are alive today are not owners of this planet but its stewards, and so have a responsibility for the long-term future of the planet and the wellbeing of future generations. A stewardship economy would be more open than an ownership economy to measures that protect the environment and we would probably be more ready than we are now to take early action when some threat to the environment is recognised. We would have a powerful practical tool to tackle environmental protection through a different way of thinking about and handling property rights in the natural world (see more in the book, *Stewardship Economy: Property rights*).

Chapter 6   Managing the environment

This book distinguishes between land (the solid surface of the planet) and the environment (the rest of the natural world including amenities, resources and sinks). The environment includes rivers, lakes and oceans which lie on the surface of the planet, the atmosphere and the electromagnetic spectrum above the surface, and what lies below the surface like mineral resources.

One reason for making the distinction between land and the environment is that it is often best for a single steward to take responsibility for a plot of land. Rights and responsibilities to the environment may need to be divided and shared amongst many.

Another reason for making the distinction is that, while title to almost all land is either established or disputed, it is only now that property rights to the environment are being allocated. We need to take action if we are to prevent the state from giving away these property rights to firms that have already staked a claim – for example by polluting the environment. Just as we need to allocate access to land at auctions that reveal the market rent of the land, we need to allocate access to the environment at auctions that reveal the resource rents of the environment.

Property rights and the price mechanism

There are many factors that influence whether people protect or exploit the environment. These include cultural, ethical and spiritual insights as well as legal and economic incentives.

Governments have four main ways to influence how we treat the environment: regulation; subsidies; taxes; property rights, including permits for extraction and emission.

All these mechanisms can play a valuable role in managing the environment. Stewardship Economy: private property without private ownership recognises property rights, and their allocation to those who purchase permits or pay the appropriate fees, fee or charge. Environmental and resource economics provide well-established - though contestable - ways to design charges and taxes that put a price on activities that damage the environment.

Property rights in the environment are currently being created and allocated by governments. This is not something with a long history that has 'stolen imperceptibly upon the world' (Thomas Paine 1797a:6) as it has with land but something that is being designed right now, even if it is not the subject of significant public debate. These property rights may offer very real opportunities to protect the environment but, in the form in which they are being introduced, may exacerbate social injustice. Governments are giving ('grandfathering') new property rights to the very firms that are currently polluting or extracting resources. In a stewardship economy the beneficiaries of resource rents are not the historic incumbents but all of us.

The experience of paying to use the environment makes it easier to recognise the logic and advantages of paying stewardship fees for the use of land. If people can see the benefits of auctioning permits as a way to control and allocate permission, for example, to discharge carbon dioxide into the environment, they may more easily see the benefits of stewardship fees as a way to allocate access to land.

Ownership economy

A system of **private property** is organised around the idea that something belongs to an individual or legal entity. This 'belonging' confers on the owner the capacity to determine the use to which the property is put.

In an **open access regime,** anyone and everyone has the right to access and use the property. There are no restrictions or limitations on who can use it and there is no individual or body that manages the way it is used.

An alternative is a system of **collective property** (state or public property) applies where the use of resources is determined by reference to the intent of the collective as a whole. No one individual makes decisions about the use of collective property without reference to this intent. Collective property, in high-consumption economies (as opposed to low-consumption, 'developing' economies) is usually held by the state, by some tier of government or its arms-length agents. In low-consumption economies it may traditionally be held by the tribe.

Common property is a third alternative and refers to property rights that are held and managed by a defined community of commoners. It is similar to collective property in that no individual member of the community has specially privileged access, but different in that those who are not commoners are excluded, and the collective has no right to be consulted. An inshore fishery is an example of a common-pool resource, where local fishermen reach some sort of agreement about their property rights – who can fish where and when, and whether there are limits on catches.

Open access regimes

In an ownership economy (the economy as we currently experience it where land is owned) an **open access regime** may be the only way to ensure that everyone has an equal right to benefit from some aspect of the environment – water supply, for example. Transferring it into private ownership may lead to more efficient use, but the benefits can then be captured by a few (the owners) rather than shared by the many (the users).

We may be reluctant to consider private property rights to the essentials of life like air and water because other forms of property (open access regimes, common property and collective property) provide some sort of prospect of fairness. We persist with open access regimes, even where they are inefficient and deleterious to the environment, because we have failed to implement fair mechanisms based in property rights and market charges.

Environmental taxes and charges

We have come to accept that we need to make at least some payments for the right to use the environment. In the UK we have the landfill tax and higher excise duty on fuel-inefficient cars, for example. If taxes on fuel are included, 7.3 per cent of all tax revenue of the UK was derived from 'green' or environmental taxes in 2006 (Select Committee on Environmental Audit (2008).

These taxes and charges increase the price of products (goods and services) that damage the environment and this in turn reduces the amount of these that we choose to buy and so the amount that is produced. All political parties in the UK are aware of the need to shift taxes away from activities we want to encourage like earnings, profits and adding value on to things that cause environmental damage. The challenge is to find ways to ensure that this burden of increased costs, particularly for domestic fuel, does not fall disproportionately on the poorer members of society.

The advantages and disadvantages of taxes compared with permits for activities which, for example, increase carbon dioxide emissions, are hotly disputed. The economic arguments are quite technical, but one of the main issues is pragmatic. If the government wants to limit emissions to the level X per year, the simplest option is to auction X permits per year and enforce their surrender when emissions take place. Firms can be expected to understand their own businesses and the cost to them of environmental protection, and so the amount that they are prepared to pay at auction for emissions permits. An alternative would be for the government to decide how much tax it needs to charge to reduce the level of demand to the equivalent of X permits per year but in most cases the government does not have enough information to set a tax at an optimal level. Taxes have been set at levels well below those needed to reduce environmental damage and numerous exceptions have been introduced to placate special interest groups. The impact of permits has also been compromised because too many permits have been issued, often as a result of special pleading. And, critically, permits have sometimes been given away in perpetuity rather than auctioned annually (more in book 2).

While, in principle, there is broad support for the appropriate use of the price mechanism, environmental taxes and tradable permits, there is still a major task to win hearts and minds for interventions that raise prices enough to make a real difference to the way we make use of the environment. One reason for this is that in an ownership economy the revenue from green charges and taxes is generally absorbed into the pool of general taxation rather than pledged (hypothecated) for some particular purpose. For this reason, many people think of them not as efficient ways to manage the environment but as 'stealth taxes' imposed by an untrustworthy government.

Governments in ownership economies are prone to soften the blow of environmental taxes through exemptions, for example those for the agricultural use of diesel fuel. The intent is understandable but the disadvantages significant. Cheap agricultural diesel at best encourages energy-inefficient agricultural practices and at worst provides the temptation for its corrupt use in road vehicles, which requires policing.

Discounts to Road Fund Tax and Congestion Charges for low-emission vehicles may be politically expedient and may play a role in raising the issue of vehicle emissions in the public consciousness. But they are less satisfactory than ensuring that the price of fuel reflects its true environmental cost, as they introduce their own distortions. Exemptions to Congestion Charges lead to increased congestion, and so to increased emissions. Discounts to Road Fund Tax provide an incentive to replace old high-emission vehicles with new low-emission ones, which can actually increase total emissions if the vehicle is being used to travel a low annual mileage. This is because the decision ignores the embedded carbon, the emissions released in the process of manufacturing the older vehicles.

Subsidies

Governments attempt to shape behaviours by providing subsidies. This may be because they believe that the subsidised goods would contribute to the common good but will be under-provided by the market as, for example, in the case of subsidies for home insulation. But it may also be the result of pressure from lobby groups, particularly from industry. Subsidies require their own bureaucracies and impose their own administrative costs, and they always run the risk of distorting markets in ways that are unintended.

Stewardship economy

The purpose of stewardship of the environment is to ensure that the environment is used efficiently and sustainably and in such a way that everyone benefits, fairly and equally. The underlying principles of stewardship are that we are stewards, not owners, of the natural world and that everyone should benefit equally from the wealth of the natural world.

To recap - the steward of an aspect of the environment has:

- the right of access – to use that aspect of the environment, for example to emit a certain amount of greenhouse gas or to extract a certain amount of water.

- the responsibility of care – to manage it responsibly and husband it for future generations, taking steps to ensure that that aspect of the environment is not damaged.

- the duty of compensation – to pay a tax to use the environment or to buy tradable permits and to surrender them when using that aspect of the environment.

Everyone is entitled to an equal share of the wealth of the environment – the 'common treasury for all mankind' (Gerrard Winstanley 1649:9) – and receives a guaranteed income in the form of an Environmental Dividend. Where resources are depleted, the wealth derived from these resources is invested for future generations.

In a stewardship economy:

The environment is held in Trust

In a stewardship economy, **Environment Stewardship Trusts** act as the trustees of each aspect of the environment and are responsible for ensuring that users of the environment make the most sustainable use of it.

If a steward damages the environment, they bear the cost. They have an incentive to care for it because they are unable to shift ('externalise') the cost of this damage to others. If their property is damaged by others, their property rights are strong enough to allow them to extract recompense for the damage from the person who caused it.

There would be an Environment Stewardship Trust at a national level for each aspect of the environment such as electromagnetic spectrum, subsoil resources, surface water, fisheries or the atmosphere. Some of these may have local subdivisions – for example a Watersheds Stewardship Trust might have a subdivision for each major watershed.

Some aspects of the environment, like the atmosphere and the oceans, need to be managed on a global scale. The description that follows is written as though in a stewardship economy global bodies such as a Sky Trust and an Oceans Trust are in existence. If it is not possible to set up these global arrangements, national Environment Stewardship Trusts could act unilaterally to tackle the use of their 'share' of the resource and make bilateral and multilateral agreements with other countries.

Environment Stewardship Trusts could take a number of possible forms. Socialists would probably like them to be state bodies; libertarians would probably see private enterprise operating a franchise as the most effective form; liberals might choose a not-for-profit or social enterprise. Commons Trusts offer the possibility of organising a Stewardship Trust for the common good but outside the remit of representative government.

Each Environment Stewardship Trust is subject to a regulatory body. When judgements about optimal levels of use of the environment are essentially political this may be a government agency. Where these judgements are of a technical, rather than political, nature it may be an independent body accountable to government, in the same way that the Bank of England is independent but accountable for keeping inflation within a range set by government.

Stewardship Trusts manage the environment

Each Environment Stewardship Trust has the task of managing its resource. It may make use of regulation (for example, setting limits to mesh sizes for fishing nets) or subsidies (for example, for home insulation) or allocation of property rights (for example by auctioning permits). In deciding its approach, and in selecting the number of permits to issue, it acts in dialogue with its regulator.

The access to the environment that it grants to stewards may take the form of private property, where the stewards are individuals, groups or businesses (for-profit and not-for-profit). It may take the form of collective property, where the stewards are government bodies (at parish, borough, city, county, regional, national, international and global levels). Or it may take the form of common property managed by a community interest company, mutual society, charity or commons trust. Only very rarely would an Environment Stewardship Trust manage any aspect of the environment as an open access regime, and in circumstances where this arrangement does not cause any environmental damage).

An Environment Stewardship Trust is subject to regulation at national and local levels. Regulatory bodies are accountable through the political structures at the level at which they operate. So, a local Environment Stewardship Trust is regulated by a local planning body, which is accountable to a Local Authority and subject to the national regulator.

Environment Stewardship Trusts issue permits

An Environment Stewardship Trust allocates property rights to the users of the environment. These property rights fall into three sorts: access, extraction and discharge (emissions or dumping).

Access. Sometimes an Environment Stewardship Trust will allocate the right to access a resource to just one user, as the Land Stewardship Trust does for each site. More usually it will want a number of users to access the resource and makes this possible by issuing permits.

Extraction of renewable or non-renewable resources. The trustee of a lake might judge that it will support a maximum of Y anglers per day and make available Y permits per day. It would be possible to limit the rate of extraction of a non-renewable resource such as oil or minerals, or a renewable resource like water, by issuing a fixed number of permits each allowing the extraction of a defined quantity during a specified time period.

Discharge (emission and dumping) Using the natural world as a sink for some sort of pollution. The trustee would issue permits that allow the discharge of a certain quantity during a defined period.

In each case a key task for the Environment Stewardship Trust is to issue **permits** – access, extraction or emission permits. These property rights are **time-limited** use-rights. People are free to buy and sell these as they are **tradable** permits, and this trading establishes a price. Permits have to be surrendered when the holder accesses that part of the environment.

The Environment Stewardship Trust needs to know how many permits to issue but it does not need to have any idea what price to put on them, as it would if it were using a taxation approach.

Permits are either auctioned or allocated equally

Once the total number of permits has been decided there are two ways in which they can be allocated.

They may be auctioned and allocated to the highest bidder. In this way the price of a permit is established in the auction. The revenue raised in the auctions is distributed to everyone on an equal per capita basis. The other approach is to divide the number of permits by the number of people and allocate as a gift an equal number of permits to each person. In this situation an 'average' user simply surrenders their permits for the resource they use. People who use less than their share can sell their unused permits to people who use more than their share. The financial consequences of the two approaches are the same, provided that the permits are tradable.

The auction approach is generally simpler and cheaper to put in to practice, particularly for 'upstream permits' and where permits for more than one sort of resource are being issued).

Permits are tradable

In a stewardship economy it would be perfectly legal to buy and sell permits. This allows those who do not need their permits to benefit from selling them, and those who need permits to acquire them. This market puts a price on the current value of a permit and ensures that whoever can make best use of the environment is able to do so. By paying for the permits, they compensate others. A futures market is likely to grow up that trades in options to buy permits. This would provide stability for users of the environment, who could secure their allocations of permits in advance, and would also reveal expectations about the future price of permits. It would, of course, also lead to speculation.

Renewable resources – the Environmental Dividend

Revenue from the sale of permits for renewable resources is distributed as an Environmental Dividend. The effect of this is that a person who uses less than their fair (equal) share of the environment receives an Environmental Dividend that outweighs their cost of using it, while a person who uses more than their fair share of the environment pays out more than they receive in Environmental Dividend.

Everyone can then see that the sole rationale for environmental permits or taxes is to establish a price and to redistribute wealth from high users to low users, rather than to raise government revenue or support government causes.

Non-renewable resources – investing resource rents

When a non-renewable resource is extracted or consumed, the revenue should, in general, not be distributed as an Environmental Dividend to those currently alive but invested for the benefit of future generations. As an example of this practice, Alaska, the Shetland Islands Council and the Norwegian government have each chosen not to spend their oil revenues but to invest them for the benefit of future generations. However, to achieve political acceptance of the scheme it may be necessary to relax this sustainability requirement for some resources and distribute the revenue as Environmental Dividend as if the resource were renewable.

No tax breaks

In a stewardship economy there are no exemptions or discounts to environmental taxes, fees or charges because these are not introduced to raise revenue but to allocate environmental resources openly and fairly. This allocation would be distorted by exemptions. So, for example, the price of agricultural diesel is the same as that of road diesel and there are no exemptions to congestion charges. That is not to argue against the government supporting agriculture or low emissions vehicles - just that they should find other ways of doing so.

Subsidies only when funded from stewardship fees

There may be a place for some subsidies in a stewardship economy. If people have only enough income to meet this week's bills, for example, the medium-term financial advantage of home insulation will have no impact while a 100 per cent grant might well do so. And governments may want to subsidise areas of research and development like renewable energy generation and greenhouse gas sequestration, although they have a patchy record of success and have failed to spot successful research and development initiatives.

If the government decides to provide subsidies, for example, to industry or charities, these should be kept to the minimum and funded from government revenue derived from stewardship fees from the land, not from environmental permits and taxes, which should be fully redistributed to everyone.

Role of government

Government would need to ensure that environmental regulation is in place at a national level, along with mechanisms to enforce the surrender of permits as required. Much of this is accomplished on their behalf by the regulators and the Environment Stewardship Trust.

Government would broker international agreements for environmental issues that cross state borders.

Environmental charges don't generate extra revenue

Suppose that an Environment Stewardship Trust identifies a new environmental issue and judges that this should be managed by requiring firms to purchase and surrender permits. This would reduce the profits that these firms make, and so the market rent that they can afford to pay for the land they use, and so the stewardship fees they pay for this land.

It may make sense to impose charges in order to reduce environmental damage, but any revenue generated will be offset by a fall in stewardship fees for land whose use is affected by the permits. Environmental charges cause Environmental Dividends to rise but the Universal Income (funded from stewardship fees) to fall. The costs of administering the environmental charges means that each environmental charge reduces the total revenue (from environmental charges and stewardship fees) by a small amount.

True cost prices

A firm that makes use of the environment has to pay a price, depending on the amount of use and the price of the permits. The purpose of the auction of environmental permits in a stewardship economy is not – as mentioned above - to raise revenue but to ensure that prices reflect the true cost of using the environment. All those in a particular industry face the same costs, as long as they are making efficient use of the environment. They pass on the costs to consumers who face a 'true cost price' (referred to by economists as the social cost) for goods and services. Consumer choices and behaviours take into account these prices, so externalities are minimised, and environmental damage is reduced.

Economic activity becomes more sustainable

Consumers facing true cost prices have a financial incentive to change their behaviour. They are likely to respond by reducing their consumption of goods and services whose production damages the environment. As they do so, economic activity shifts from the unsustainable to the sustainable.

People pay for the use they make of the environment

For renewable resources, the Environmental Dividend ensures that wealth is transferred from high per capita users of the environment to low per capita users. For non-renewable resources, high users contribute most to the fund for investment for future generations

Chapter 7   Amenities & resources

Amenities are resources that people enjoy directly. A site may serve as an amenity either if it can be accessed by the public or if it benefits sites nearby. What prevents amenities from being overused? How should their upkeep be financed? After defining the nature of sustainable development and the range of amenities and resources to be considered, this chapter contrasts how these are managed in ownership and stewardship economies.

The following chapters discuss the cases of pollution (Chapter 8) and climate change (Chapter 9).

Sustainable development

David Brower, the American environmental campaigner and founder of Friends of the Earth, famously said 'We do not inherit the earth from our fathers, we are borrowing it from our children', apparently drawing on a Native American saying. He later said that the sentiments he wished to be remembered for were more extreme: 'We're not just borrowing from our children, we're stealing from them – and it's not even considered to be a crime.'

The idea that we should maintain, not deplete, the stock of wealth available for future generations lies at the heart of the idea of sustainable development – 'development that meets the needs of the present without compromising the ability of future generations to meet their own needs' (World Commission for Development & Environment of the UN 1987) (quoted in David Pearce 1993).

For renewable resources the meaning of this definition is clear: we should, for example, not measurably lower the water table, deplete the topsoil or reduce the stocks of pollinators or fish. For non-renewable resources it could be interpreted as meaning that each generation must leave available as much oil, copper and so on as they inherited. But such a strong interpretation of sustainability assumes that one form of capital cannot substitute for another. It would totally rule out the extraction of a wide range of non-renewable resources like oil and minerals.

A weak interpretation of sustainability is that the depletion of non-renewable resources can be offset by any investment in new physical or human capital. A practical, middle-ground, interpretation is that the stock of the resource and its substitutes must be maintained indefinitely. This approach recognises certain critical assets are irreplaceable (Kirk Hamilton 2006:123) but allows extraction at the rate at which substitutes are produced, or the resource itself re-used and re-cycled.

Ecosystem services

Ecosystem services are 'services provided by the natural environment that benefit people' (Defra 2007:3), both by contributing to the generation of income, enhancing wellbeing and preventing damage to society. A garden that absorbs rainwater is contributing to the prevention of costly floods, an ecosystem with rich biodiversity may be the source of new drugs or new species of agricultural value.

This anthropocentric concept has been developed to meet the challenge of including in cost-benefit studies the benefits provided by the environment that are freely available and so are not traded in the market place. We need to put a value on these benefits because if we are to use the rationale of economics we have to be able to quantify the economic reasons for investing in environmental protection. If we fail to invest to protect these environmental assets there will be costs that fall elsewhere (externalities) and we will have to invest in an alternative way to provide the service.

The Millennium Ecosystem Assessment (2003, 2005) was a partnership of UN agencies, international scientific organizations, and development agencies. Its reports provided a framework for classifying the benefits we derive from the environment into four broad categories:

- 'Cultural services'. The environmental assets that provide cultural services are amenities. These are places that people enjoy directly – nature as a place to walk, play, learn, engage in sport or just be because of its intrinsic qualities – landscape, peace, calm, spirituality, wildlife, naturalness.

- 'Provisioning services'. The environmental assets that provide provisioning services are natural resources, both renewable and non-renewable, that may be extracted and used away from the resource site. These include the examples of water, fish and minerals described later in this chapter and also things that are even more difficult to price such as natural medicines, biochemicals and biodiversity (plant and animal species and varieties, genetic resources).

- 'Supporting services' – those that underlie all other ecosystem processes including soil formation, photosynthesis, pollination, nutrient cycling and water cycling.

- 'Regulating services' – environmental assets and processes that often are very complex and regulate aspects of the ecosystem such as air quality, water flows, erosion, diseases, pests, natural hazards, pollination, water purification and climate control. These include sinks that are able to absorb and process a certain amount of pollution when it is discharged (emitted or dumped).

There is no reason why these categories need to be limited to such an anthropocentric concept, and benefits may be judged according to the impact on the whole ecosystem – not just humans.

Environmental problems can be prioritised on the basis of a quantitative estimate of the extent to which sustainability standards are exceeded and the costs of the measures required to meet the standards. Rofie Hueting and colleagues published a paper for CBS Statistics Netherlands and the World Wildlife Fund on Environmentally Sustainable National Income (1992:24). The authors identified the then top priorities as: climate change; depletion of the ozone layer; depletion of natural resources; photochemical smog (ground level ozone); acidification (acid rain); dissemination of toxic chemicals; eutrophication (excess of nutrients in bodies of water that lead to algal blooms); amenity use of the landscape; desiccation and soil pollution. There are probably other priorities that we would now add, including the loss of pollinators.

This chapter points to some of the current difficulties in protecting and optimising the use of environmental resources in ownership economies and shows how it would be possible to manage amenities and natural resources in a stewardship economy.

Ownership economy

Amenities

Amenity sites would often command a higher market rent and market value if they were put to some other use, for example as a site for residential or commercial use. Where this is the case, it can only be prevented in a market economy by means of regulations such as those imposed by planning authorities.

Site with public access

The responsibility for upkeep of an amenity site falls on its owner who acts out of a mixture of self-interest and a sense of responsibility – either to the public or to the place itself. Such a benevolent landowner may be a private owner, a charity or an arm of government.

Landowners may resist access to their land because if they, for example, permit access, to ramblers they forfeit the benefits of privacy and exclusive use, they may risk legal action if a walker is injured and may have to bear the costs of footpath maintenance and damage. Public rights of way across an estate may reduce its value – indeed this formed the grounds of appeal against the Community Rights of Way Act to the European Count of Human Rights (Guardian 10/11/01).

Site that can be appreciated from nearby

Some sites – for example parks, green spaces, rivers or the ocean – enhance the value of neighbouring sites that overlook them or are close enough to provide easy access.

The purchaser of a site with a good view or a nearby park pays a premium which they expect to recoup when they sell it. There are ways in which we do use this enhanced value to support the amenity site, for example, the Old State House in Connecticut is preserved by taxing each of the 2,753 windows that look out onto it from neighbouring buildings (Stewart Brand 1994/1995:96).

Renewable resources

Sustainability is linked to the natural regenerative capacity of the environment. The sustainability standard of a substance in the environment is the level (stock) that can be maintained indefinitely. The admissible burden is the rate (flow) at which it can be introduced into or withdrawn from the environment – the annual budget for that substance.

Environmental economists have developed methodologies for valuing environmental assets that are complicated, costly and time-consuming to carry out rigorously. They are always contestable as they depend on subjective estimates from individuals such as the reported 'willingness to pay'. These rely on each respondent understanding the environmental good in the same way and are difficult to elicit without introducing several sorts of bias. Valuations are also contestable because the non-linear behaviour of complex systems means that there are major uncertainties about the risk of extreme and sudden changes like ecosystem failure.

Most of the time we can only put good-enough costs on the use of the environment, but even using estimates is better than excluding the costs on the grounds that they are too difficult to measure. The challenge is to find ways to ensure that the beneficiaries pay these costs instead of treating the environment as a free good. The examples of renewable resources discussed in this section include water, fish, forests and topsoil, though the same principles and methods can be applied to other resources.

Water

The discussion of water that follows focuses on national issues – the challenges of managing water resources that cross national boundaries are discussed elsewhere.

Use and availability of water

Rivers are drying up around the world, and the water table in many aquifers is falling. In high-consumption economies we use about 150 litres per day in each of our homes, and about 100 litres per day is lost in leakage in its supply. But we consume far more as the embedded 'virtual water' contained in our food and clothing – it takes 100 litres to produce a portion of rice, 150 litres for a round of toast, 1000 litres for a glass of milk, 3000 litres for a hamburger and 8000 litres for the cotton to make a T-shirt. We are each responsible for using about 30 times more water than is piped into our homes (Fred Pearce 2006:21).

This situation has been driven by economic development and by one of the success stories of technology – the 'green revolution'. New crop varieties introduced over the last half century have enabled food production to keep up with population growth. But these varieties require more fertiliser and water than the traditional ones. Agriculture accounts for more than 70 per cent of freshwater use globally, while in the USA power generation accounts for about 40 per cent of water use, either from cooling or from evaporation from reservoirs (Economist 2016, November 5th : 21-22) .

As is well known, climate change means that the climate will become less predictable. Increased rainfall is anticipated in northern latitudes, central Africa and east Asia. Moderate droughts are predicted to double in southern Europe, North Africa, the USA and western Eurasia during the next century. Nearly a third of the land area of the world may be at risk of extreme drought by the end of the century, compared with 1 per cent at present (Eleanor Burke et al 2006). Restricted access to water is likely to give rise to significant population movements and conflict in the 21st century.

Water management

Northern Bangladesh is the wettest place on earth, but its people suffer frequent water shortages. Problems with water very often lie not in the supply but in the approach to water management.

Water is often managed as an open access regime. This has the advantage that everyone, even the very poor, has access to this life-sustaining resource. The disadvantage is that water has been used wastefully and inefficiently because it is under-priced. Where there is open access to surface water there are often no penalties for contaminating it, which leads to failures of water quality and consequent health problems.

There have, by contrast, been many examples over the last 5000 years in rural economies where water resources have been very efficiently managed as a common pool resource (Elinor Ostrom, 1990). Social institutions have been developed to share the available water, particularly where the construction of collection and distribution systems has required collective effort. When a village shares out its available water, people have ways of monitoring what is going on and challenging the process if it does not seem fair.

However, in low-consumption economies where water is scarce and localised, it has often been allocated as the gift of the powerful and used to reinforce that power. And in high-consumption economies it is often those who have an historical claim who have privileged access. In high-consumption economies people have traditionally paid for water but not in a way that reflects the amount they use, and this creates what is effectively an open access regime. In times of drought, water may be managed as common property through hosepipe bans and other restrictions on unnecessary use.

Where domestic water metering has been introduced, users have a price signal that influences their water usage. This leads households to reduce water use and may provide the incentive to use water of different qualities for different purposes – rainwater for bathing, purified water for drinking and so on. But metering is regressive – the shift from fixed charges based on property values in the UK has shifted costs from the rich to the poor who spend a greater proportion of their income on water even though their per capita consumption is lower (National Energy Action, 2019).

In almost all economies water for agriculture and industry is supplied at a price that is far below its true cost, either because these bulk users have negotiated low prices or because they are heavily subsidised. This has encouraged wasteful practices, including the planting of crops that are unsuitable for the area because of the high water requirements. This may boost economic development in the short run but, if the water assets are not managed sustainably, it depletes natural capital and damages economic growth in the long-term.

Dams

One response to water shortages, as well as to flood control and the need for hydroelectric power, is dam-building. Large dams have economic, social and environmental costs which include the loss of farmland, wetlands, fisheries and habitats. Submerged vegetation releases methane. Species dependent on bodies of still water proliferate – anopheles mosquitoes and freshwater snails are examples particularly harmful to human health. Any area lost by submersion will contain sites to which people may have strong emotional and spiritual connections as well as economic value. Dams have a limited life as they silt up, are outflanked by erosion of the valley walls, or are breached by floods. Irrigated land may succumb to salination or be devastated by structural failure of the dam. Hydro power can be effective without large dams, but it is less efficient and lacks storage capacity, making run-of-river generation particularly vulnerable to drought.

Even when the benefits of a new dam are considered to outweigh the costs, some people gain (including the owners of land coming under irrigation) at the expense of others (including those who depend on the areas to be submerged, and those deprived of water who live far downstream). In low-consumption economies people who are dependent on the land may have no recognised title, even if they have customary rights. Construction of a dam may result in this group being evicted or deprived of water without compensation. Even those with recognised legal title may find their land compulsorily purchased at a price over which they have no control.

Wells & Boreholes

If water is extracted from an aquifer faster than it is replenished, as in the case of about 20 per cent of the world's aquifers, the water table falls. Shallow wells and boreholes dry up, water becomes more difficult to access and the aquifer's ability to store water is damaged. In coastal regions sea water intrudes into the coastal water table which is degraded by salination. If an aquifer is managed sustainably, water is extracted at the same rate at which the aquifer is replenished.

Fisheries

A commercial fishery should be aiming to fish in such a way that fish stocks are not seriously depleted. Natural populations of fish are known to fluctuate unpredictably, behaviour that is also found in dynamic computer models of predator-prey relationships but not in simple computer models of fish stocks. There is a danger that simple models may underestimate the risk that a given level of catch will cause extinction, or near extinction, of the fish.

Overfishing has decimated many species of fish. The underlying cause is that fishing in the oceans and even some rivers was for a long time managed as an open access regime. Action has been taken to reduce overfishing by managing these fisheries as common property – that is to say, agreements have been reached about mesh sizes, fishing seasons and eventually about maximum permitted catches. These have been translated into national quotas through international negotiations, and the quotas treated as private property rights.

In spite of some successes there are a range of criticisms that can be levelled: agreement on catch quotas has often lagged behind the scientific understanding – action has been reactive rather than pro-active; while some quotas have been appropriately time-limited, others appear to be indefinite, or, at best, ambiguous, in duration; the

80

allocation of quotas has reflected the bargaining position of the participating nations and their historical claims; some nations, including the UK, have given their quotas to the individual fishermen who had been using this natural resource in the years before the quotas were introduced. This approach to allocation, 'grandfathering', favoured those particular individuals and ignores all others who might want to fish, or indeed the wider community.

Quotas have been treated as de facto private property rights. Having been bought and sold several times, the very unequal holdings seem unfair to many – particularly when they have been bought by foreign boats. There is no agreed underlying ethical basis for this allocation of the available property rights as quotas, and thus no principle to refer to in difficult cases both now and in the future. Is it right, for example, that land-locked states should for all time have no claim on the wealth of the seas? In addition, quotas are not adequately policed, and it is difficult to do so.

Large quantities of dead fish have been discarded by fishermen because they do not have the permits required to land them.

Whaling

The purpose of the International Whaling Commission is to conserve whales for commercial fishing. In 1986 it agreed a moratorium on commercial whaling, from which Norway and Iceland opted out. Whale populations have recovered slowly since this moratorium was adopted, and the time may come when the Commission decides to withdraw it. It would be unfair and inefficient if the Commission were to gift (grandfather) whaling rights to countries that have in the past been whaling nations.

Deforestation

Financial incentives encourage logging rather than conservation of natural forests. Owners, tenants and criminals may all profit from the sale of timber or from the agricultural use of cleared land. They do not often directly experience the costs of the loss of natural capital including the rapid loss of soil fertility, loss of ecosystem services, rapid run-off causing flooding, sediment deposits in reservoirs and local climate change such as reduction in rainfall. They do not experience any financial cost arising from the release of greenhouse gases by deforestation.

Soil quality and erosion

Land degradation in Africa and Central Asia is a major challenge to the international community (Millennium Economic Assessment 2005), with 25 million acres degraded or lost each year. The main problems are desertification due to deforestation and farming, and salination due to irrigation. Nearly 70 per cent of the natural capital of low-consumption economies currently lies in their cropland and pastureland (Kirk Hamilton, 2007). It is critically important to maintain the quality of the few inches of topsoil on which our life, and particularly our food supply, depends.

Non-renewable (exhaustible) resources

Our management of non-renewable resources falls short of any of the interpretations of sustainable development. We impose few limits beyond the cost of extraction and local planning restrictions. The cost of resource depletion has been borne by the environment not by firms – the costs have been externalised – and resources have been depleted more rapidly than is wise. The agreements made from time to time by the Organisation of Petroleum Exporting Countries (OPEC) to limit the rate of production of oil is one of the few examples of a concerted attempt to control the rate of extraction of a natural resource, but this was for short-term financial and political reasons, not for environmental considerations.

Environmental economists have demonstrated that consumption can be maintained at the highest sustainable level if the revenue (resource rent) obtained from resource extraction is invested in alternative forms of capital, for example, research and development in alternative materials or renewable energy. There are few examples where this has been carried out in practice, not least because these resource rents are normally captured by commercial firms.

Stewardship economy

Stewardship provides practical ways to tackle many of the challenges set out above.

Amenities – a site with public access

Rents

If a steward grants access by the public to their land this will generally reduce the market rent of their land and so the stewardship fees that they pay. The public is in effect providing a subsidy to the steward to compensate them for the access they provide.

Planning

Planning restrictions may include a public right of access, reducing the desirability of land and so its market rent. In a stewardship economy this is reflected in a compensatory fall in the stewardship fees.

Negative stewardship fees (subsidies)

If planning requirements are onerous, and there are no positive bids for the land when it changes hands, the Land Stewardship Trust may invite negative bids for a stewardship fees that will act as a subsidy for meeting the planning requirements and maintaining the amenity – stewardship support fees - how much do you need to be paid to take this piece of land? And the lowest bidder gets it.

Amenities – a site that can be appreciated from nearby

In a stewardship economy the steward automatically pays fees that reflect the value contributed by a nearby amenity that benefits their own site. If it is judged that an amenity site is worthy of financial support it would be possible to estimate the premiums paid in their stewardship fees by neighbouring sites, and to earmark (hypothecate) all or some of the income to be paid to the steward of the amenity site. As examples of renewable resources this section considers the management of water, fish, forests and topsoil.

Watershed Stewardship Trust

The European Water Framework Directive has identified 11 River Basin Districts in England and Wales, each centred on one or more major rivers and including their estuaries and the adjacent coastline. In a stewardship economy each of these would be served by a Watershed Stewardship Trust which is the local office of the national Watersheds Stewardship Trust. It holds surface and ground water resources in Trust and is responsible for the sustainable management of these resources.

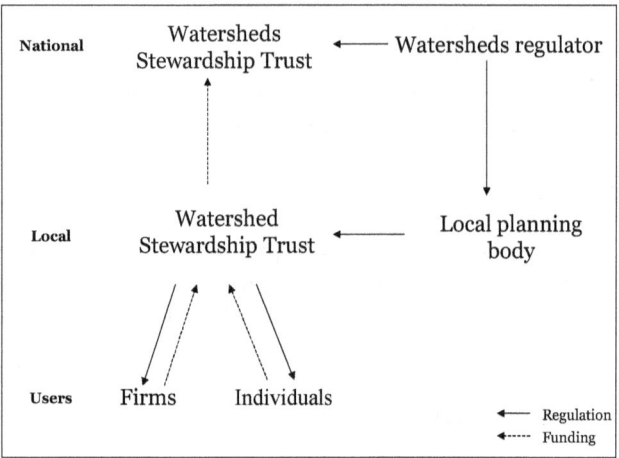

The Watersheds Stewardship Trust is subject to regulation at national and local levels. Regulatory bodies are accountable through the political structures at the level at which they operate. So, the local Watershed Stewardship Trust is regulated by a local planning body, which is accountable to a Local Authority and subject to the national regulator.

The watersheds regulator identifies, for renewable water resources, an acceptable range within which stocks of water – levels in rivers, lakes and aquifers – should lie as well as environmental standards and levels of charges.

The Watershed Stewardship Trust makes its resources – such as amenities, wildlife, navigation, fishing and piped water – available to multiple end-users through some combination of regulation, negotiation with stakeholders and issuing permits. If it fails to maintain the standards set by the regulator it is liable to a penalty equal to the value of any damage or disimprovement.

The Watershed Stewardship Trust may make regulations for the use of water resources, in addition to those set by the regulatory body. It might for example restrict access to an amenity site during nesting time, or control permissible discharges from boats.

Where there are many claims on the use of surface water, such as a reservoir, the Watershed Stewardship Trust may manage it as common property in negotiation with stakeholders.

The Watershed Stewardship Trust may require everyone who uses water to purchase and surrender permits for the use they make of it.

To do so the Watershed Stewardship Trust first identifies the maximum rate of sustainable use. This might be the maximum total daily visitor numbers to an amenity site, the maximum total annual amount of a pollutant that can be discharged per year into a sink or the total volume of water that the can be sustainably extracted per year (the water budget). These limits may be provided by the regulatory body.

Next, it divides the total into permits of practical size – which might be, for example, a permit to allow one person entry to an amenity site for a day; a permit to allow a polluter to emit a defined amount of the pollutant during the course of a particular year; or a permit to allow a utility company to extract a certain volume of water in a particular year.

It then makes these permits available. It would not want to give these away, whether to its favourites or on a first-come-first-served basis, as a market or black market would develop, and the recipients of the gifts (and the dealers) would reap the benefit. Rather it would either auction the permits or set a price that ensures that most of the permits are sold.

Anyone who buys a permit becomes a steward of their share of the resource – they have a tradable private property right and their purchase compensates others. Businesses then pass these costs on to consumers. Permits can be saved into the future, which prevents waste at the end of the year. The income from the sale of permits is distributed to everyone as an Environmental Dividend. The balance between permits, regulation and negotiation is a matter for the Watershed Stewardship Trust to decide.

This method of allocation would apply in a steady-state stewardship economy. Transition to a stewardship economy would begin from the starting point of respect for existing property rights in environmental goods.

In a stewardship economy the water supply companies pass the costs of their permits on to their end-users. They are required to do so without the cross-subsidisation of industry and agriculture by domestic customers with which we are familiar in ownership economies. Everyone who makes use of a natural resource like water then pays a price that reflects the full cost to the environment, so the price of a slice of toast or the cotton in a T-shirt is a true cost price that reflects the cost of the embedded virtual water. This leads to more efficient water use and lower demand, for example in agriculture a move from sprinkler irrigation to drip irrigation and the use of more drought-resistant varieties.

Domestic use accounts for only a small proportion of all the water used, but domestic water pricing needs to be handled with care as water is, of course, essential for life and health. true cost pricing, with the revenue shared out as an equal per capita Environmental Dividend, ensures that those who use more than their fair, equal, share pay compensation to those who use less. This results in most cases in a payment from rich to poor.

In low-consumption economies agriculture can account for 75-90 per cent of all the water used, and in high-consumption economies industry, particularly energy generation, is a heavy user, while 30 to 60 per cent is lost through leakage. True cost pricing would lead to change in the practice of water companies, industry and agriculture.

Stewardship brings with it an expectation that, in addition to true cost pricing, environmental impact assessments and cost benefit analyses will be undertaken fairly and transparently for any infrastructure development. Large dam projects in stewardship economies would have to pay their full environmental costs and are less likely to be built than in ownership economies. People whose land suffers are automatically compensated by a fall in their stewardship fees. People whose land benefits from the dam automatically pay higher stewardship fees, and this revenue may be used to contribute to financing the construction of the dam.

The builder of the dam is required to purchase any buildings and other improvements in the area to be flooded for their Depreciated

Replacement Cost, which compensates owners for their past investments. Although displaced from their land, these former occupants are in a position to bid for access to other land of their choice and anyone subject to this sort of compulsory purchase should be given additional compensation to facilitate this bidding and removal.

Wells and boreholes are managed sustainably. A falling water table is treated as a disimprovement, assessed by Watershed Stewardship Trust and the disimprovement value charged to the stewards responsible. The Watershed Stewardship Trust is itself held accountable by its regulator and has to invest disimprovement fees collected for future generations.

Efficient rainwater harvesting and small-scale water collection schemes are encouraged in a stewardship economy. Higher water prices justify the investment needed for locally appropriate rainwater harvesting and storage mechanisms.

Small dams, particularly those that fill only seasonally, contribute to the prevention of flooding, and the silt they collect retains moisture and supports agriculture. They are treated as improvements, not disimprovements. Desalination of sea water becomes a commercially more attractive proposition as water fetches a higher price than in an ownership economy, though in a stewardship economy energy costs are also higher.

Pollution of aquifers, including salination, is handled in the same way as pollution of land. The volume of pollutants that the aquifer is capable of handling sustainably are managed by permits, while for irreversible change the polluter is liable to pay the disimprovement value to the Environmental Stewardship Trust.

Fisheries

Fisheries differ one from another and deciding a policy for each fishery requires a dialogue between scientists, conservationists and fishermen to craft a locally appropriate approach. In a stewardship economy, the basis for this might be that:

- Fishing rights in the oceans are managed neither as open access regimes nor as common property regimes but as private property rights. A fisheries regulator is responsible for making an assessment of a safe yearly catch compatible with maintaining sustainable fish populations. An Oceans Stewardship Trust (or a

Watershed Stewardship Trust for inland fisheries) creates private property rights in the form of tradable permits to extract that quantity of fish each year. It also ensures that these quotas are not exceeded.

- The Stewardship Trust allocates permits at auction. Existing historical claims and political dealing are irrelevant to this allocation. The extraction permits are tradable, so fishermen who inadvertently catch more than their quota can buy permits to cover this catch; and can provide themselves with stability by purchasing options for future years.

The design of permits is important. The system can become self-policing if fishermen own a financial asset that rises in value provided that everyone fishes sustainably. The permits may therefore need to be allocated on a rolling basis perhaps 5-10 years ahead, and to represent a proportion of the total safe yearly catch rather than a tonnage. This arrangement ensures that the annual value of a permit rises over its lifetime if fish stocks increase.

If the Stewardship Trust allows overfishing that reduces fish stocks, the measure of the damage it has done is the difference between the value of the fish that are landed and the fish that would have been landed if stocks had not been depleted. The Stewardship Trust is liable to pay this disimprovement value to the regulator. This sum is invested for the benefit of future generations, to reflect the fact that this potentially renewable resource has been permanently depleted.

The total annual amount bid for the permits, minus the running costs of the Oceans (or Watershed) Stewardship Trust, represents the total revenue from the fishing rights of the oceans (or rivers). This is available for distribution as an Environmental Dividend.

The main advantages of this sort of approach are that

- Fishing rights are available to those who most value them (or at least to those who are able to pay the most for them).

- Everyone who does not have fishing rights is compensated.

- There is an understandable ethical basis for sharing out the available natural wealth.

- The incentives work to conserve fish stocks (and preserve a long-term high rate of extraction).

- If a boat is unable to fish, its owner can sell or lease out its permits.

- If a boat lands more than its quota its owner can buy permits to cover their catch, which should make it more profitable to sell the catch legally rather than to dump it or sell it illegally.

- If this approach is to result in genuine conservation, the system of permits has to be policed more effectively than the European fish quotas.

An alternative option would be for the fisheries to be managed as a commons trust and quotas or fishing restrictions agreed by mutual agreement of those identified as commoners.

Whaling

Whaling could be controlled by issuing and auctioning permits. However, there is controversy about whaling, and it might be that both whalers and conservationists would bid for the permits that become available. Conservationists could control the volume of whaling by buying and retiring permits. This approach would be open to conservationists for any aspect of the environment.

The International Whaling Commission might, or course, consider this proposal unsatisfactory and be tempted to game the system by issuing extra permits for the next auction. This would need transparent public discussion.

Forests

In a stewardship economy the costs of deforestation are not shifted to others (externalised). Loss of trees, topsoil and ecosystem services like biodiversity conservation are all assessed by the Land Stewardship Trust as a loss of natural capital (disimprovements to the site) and charged to the steward of that site. The impact that local damage such as flooding, droughts and silting has on the stewardship fees of nearby sites are also assessed and charged to the steward of the forest. And in an established stewardship economy the assumption is that all emitters of greenhouse gases require permits for their release, including that generated by deforestation.

Economic instruments may have perverse consequences when people are prepared to act illegally to evade them – the landfill tax in the UK stimulates illegal fly-tipping, for example. The illegal logging that makes up a large part of the problem of deforestation in some tropical forests is not currently controlled by regulations because these are unenforceable. The rule of law and enforceable property rights are one part of the solution. But it may be necessary to make available international funding to enable governments to police the protection of forests. It might be possible to subsidise the management of forests by placing 'conservation easements' on sites whose stewards are committed to preserving the forest and are willing to combat illegal logging on the land.

Commercial plantations differ from natural forests in that they are intended to be felled and re-planted. In a stewardship economy trees in a commercial forestry operation are treated as a crop that is wholly owned by the steward, and no disimprovement charges are made when they are cut down).

Soil quality and erosion

When it transfers the stewardship of a site, the Land Stewardship Trust needs to make a valuation of any soil erosion, which is a form of disimprovement to a site. If the Trust is aware that some locations are at particular risk of soil erosion it will need to make more regular valuations, perhaps yearly. In either case it will revalue and collect the disimprovement value from the steward. This is an example of the way that the day-to-day operation of stewardship plays a major role in promoting sustainable management of land and the environment.

In areas where irrigation may lead to destruction of soil fertility from salinity, the Land Stewardship Trust has the responsibility of monitoring salinity and quantifying the cost of the damage. This has to be paid by the steward, who internalises these costs and is provided with a financial incentive to avoid soil destruction. The revenue is invested by the Stewardship Trust for future generations. The process provides land users with an incentive to prevent the salination and quantifies the costs of irrigation schemes.

Environmental Dividend

Compensation for the sustainable use of renewable resources is achieved by distributing the revenue from the sale of permits equally to everyone as an Environmental Dividend. Users of renewable resources have to pay more for the resource they use than in an ownership economy, but a person who uses their fair (equal) share is exactly compensated by receiving their share of the Environmental Dividend. Those who use more than their fair (equal) share make a net additional payment in a stewardship economy, after allowing for the Environmental Dividend, while those who use less are net beneficiaries.

Non-renewable (exhaustible) resources

If a firm in a stewardship economy wants to extract minerals, the steward or tenant of the land that must provide access and space for the necessary improvements like pit-head equipment. This use of the land must be compliant with local planning regulations, which may impose restrictions on vehicle movements or even on the maximum permitted rate of extraction that is compatible with the local environment.

The firm may also have to purchase and surrender extraction permits which are managed by a national Subsoil Stewardship Trust. If the Trust believes that there is a need to limit the national rate of extraction, it may use an appropriate mix of regulation and negotiation as well as the regular auction of permits.

This approach relies on:

- Extraction firms paying for extraction permits and passing these costs on to the consumer.

- Higher prices reducing consumer demand.

- Revenue from the sales of permits being reinvested in other forms of capital for the benefit of future generations, for example, in research and development in alternative materials or renewable energy.

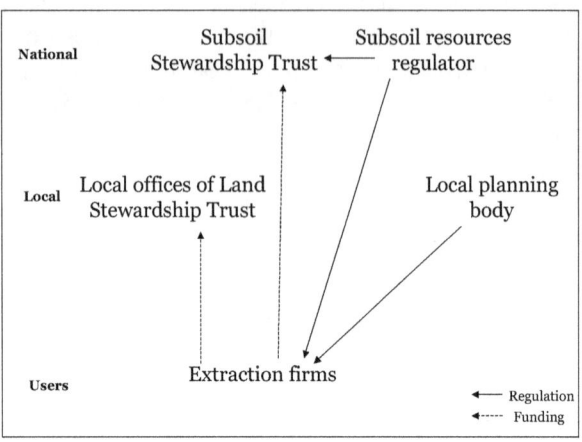

A regulatory body decides on an appropriate national rate of extraction and the Subsoil Stewardship Trust auctions the appropriate number of permits for that year. The number of permits made available each year, as well as the level of demand, determines the price that the permits fetch and the total revenue generated. The same approach applies not just to minerals but to other subsoil resources like oil, and to mineral resources on or below the ocean bed.

Investment for future generations

The essential requirement to achieve sustainability (in the middle-ground sense of maintaining the stock of resources or their substitutes) is that the revenue from non-renewable resources is not distributed as an Environmental Dividend; rather, it is invested to provide substitutable physical or even social capital for the benefit of future generations.

Socialists might like to see the government making these investments directly. Liberals might like to see the revenue used to purchase shares in suitable new private ventures. Libertarians might favour distribution as an Environmental Dividend and rely on individuals to invest it appropriately.

In spite of these good theoretical reasons for investing the revenue from the extraction of non-renewable resources, there are practical reasons why it may sometimes be necessary to distribute it as an Environmental Dividend. One is a matter of governance; where there is a high risk that funds made available for investment in alternatives may be diverted by corrupt actors. Another reason is that this is the most direct and transparent way to compensate the poor for the introduction of environmental protection. It may be essential in the short term to achieve realistic pricing of greenhouse gas emissions.

The impact of true cost pricing on firms

Each firm is able to pass on the average level of environmental cost to their consumers in a true cost price for their goods and services, so the only firms that are penalised directly are those that cause greater environmental damage than the average for their industry. The goods and services provided by an industry that damages the environment are, however, more expensive than they would be in the absence of true cost pricing and this reduces the demand for these products and the amount produced.

To recap -

A stewardship economy would have a major impact on the way we deal with the environment. It would

- improve access to land by the public

- provide subsidies to amenity sites

- improve the management of renewable resources by establishing private property rights and true cost prices

- redistribute wealth from those who use more than their fair share of the environment to those who use less than their fair share, by means of the Environmental Dividend

- invest on behalf of future generations to compensate them for the non-renewable resources we extract and the environmental damage we cause.

Chapter 8   Pollution

This chapter considers how pollution is affected by property rights. It explores how stewardship discourages pollution of a single site and pollution of neighbouring sites. The following chapter will explore how stewardship influences climate change, as an example of pollution with a global impact.

Pollution becomes a problem when the Earth's ecosystems are unable to absorb the pollutants we produce without sustaining damage. Degradation of the environment has become a pressing problem over the last two centuries as a result of population growth and increasing standards of living.   As per capita GDP rises, pollution may:

- fall – e.g., pollution of groundwater by sewage
- rise then fall – e.g., air pollution
- rise apparently inexorably – e.g., household waste, CO_2.

Ownership economy

Land ownership provides a feeble incentive to minimise pollution, whether this is pollution of a single site or exported pollution. This is exacerbated by the way in which we discount the importance of pollution on the grounds that its consequences are not felt now but in the future.

Damage on a single site

When a firm rents a site from a landlord and pollutes it, the landlord will take action to protect the value of their asset. This may include eviction, applying pressure on the firm to remedy the pollution or seeking compensation for the damage.

Where the firm owns the site and there is no external landlord, however, there may be no immediate financial reason to take note of damage to the land. This is because the cost of owning land is not experienced as current expenditure but as a past financial outlay. If the value of the land is reduced by pollution, the owner will not experience any consequence in this year's accounts unless these are drawn up on an accruals basis. There is no incentive to record this reduction in value as a loss. And the market value of land tends to rise over the years, which masks any loss in value due to the pollution.

The state, most notoriously in Eastern Europe, has often proved to be a bad landlord in this respect, simply ignoring pollution and environmental degradation of its land. This is particularly the case for military installations and the nuclear industry.

Impact on neighbouring sites

Pollution may be exported beyond the boundaries of the site used by the polluter. The three main categories of such pollution are:

- **air pollution**, particularly particulates and lead from petrol

- **water pollution**, including nitrates from fertiliser use and contamination by sewage

- **toxic chemicals** including pesticides, heavy metals and radionucleotides which may be released during current production (either planned discharges or accidental spills) or from storage dumps.

These give rise to costs that are, in an ownership economy, borne by other landowners near and far. The costs of heavy metal contamination in the area around an industrial site or nuclear fallout on land at some distance from nuclear disasters such as Windscale, Chernobyl and Fukushima are not borne by the polluters. The Broads Authority has had to pay for the clean-up of the Norfolk and Suffolk Broads following run-off of nitrate fertilisers into streams and rivers.

Pollution of neighbouring sites can be discouraged in an ownership economy by imposing costs on the polluter, either as regulatory penalties or as legal damages under tort law including the Land Compensation Act (1973). But the potential costs means that many of those affected do not take this legal route.

Discounting the future

The costs of reducing (abating) pollution are paid now, while the benefits are felt in the future. How important do we think this future is? In our economic decisions most of us do not value the future as much as the present – we discount the future. If you are offered the choice between £100 today or £100 in a year's time you will probably take the money now. This may be because you want to spend it now, not later. But even if you don't want to spend it you might be able to invest it at a real interest rate of 1 per cent, in which case the offer of £100 in a year's time is worth £1 less. In this case we are discounting the future by the real interest rate of 1 per cent.

We usually assume that discounting is exponential, that is to say the value falls by the same proportion each year. After 100 years, with a discount rate of 5 per cent, the value of the future is less than 1 per cent of present value; even when the discount rate is 1 per cent the future is worth only 37 per cent of present value. This means that it is difficult to attach any value to what happens in 100 years' time unless the discount rate is far below the real, let alone the nominal, interest rate. That makes it very difficult to justify any investment now that might produce even very great advantages if these are centuries away.

Discounting is only appropriate for situations where change is continuous and there are low levels of uncertainty, which is not the case for many environmental issues. There has been increasing support among environmental economists, particularly following the Stern review of climate change (Nicholas Stern 2007), for the proposition that long-term discount rates should be much lower than real interest rates. H M Treasury's Green Book (H M Treasury 2007:98) proposed that cost-benefit analysis for infrastructure projects should use a discount rate of 3.5 per cent for costs and benefits accruing up to 30 years, falling to 1 per cent when looking more than 300 years in the future. From an environmental perspective even these values seem far too high.

Ecosystems are constantly changing, their members co-evolving. Individual species come and go. Ecosystems may grow but they are vulnerable to collapse, even after hundreds of generations of apparent stability. Greens who see long-term ecosystem health as the ultimate priority, and some people of faith, will use a discount rate for environmental decisions of zero, or close to zero. This is equivalent to deciding to use the environment only to the extent that the long-term health of the ecosystem is not harmed.

Take, as an example, the safe management of nuclear waste. An environmental economist using the government's preferred rates in the Green Book would discount future costs and risks and judge them to be negligible if they will be incurred in over 100 years' time. A green might ask whether the legacy of nuclear waste with a half-life of thousands or even millions of years is a cost worth incurring to supply us with electricity for the next thirty years.

In an ownership economy there are no automatic mechanisms to reflect back to firms the cost of the damage they are doing to the environment. Costs that will be incurred in the future are heavily discounted and therefore easy to ignore.

Stewardship economy

Husbandry clauses

There is a tradition of clauses in English agricultural leases, going back at least to the early 18th century (Jonty Williams 2014:7), legally binding the tenant to various methods of 'good husbandry'.

An essential feature of stewardship is that the right to occupy and use land is balanced by the responsibility to care for it. This responsibility, set out in specific husbandry clauses, ensures that the steward is responsible for any damage or disimprovement. In this way stewardship raises the profile in economic decision-making of disimprovements to the land.

Jonty Williams believes that all forms of tenure – rural and urban, leasehold and freehold – need to have legally binding husbandry clauses (Jonty Williams 2014:16) that might cover issues from the removal of thistles (Jonty Williams 2014:24) to rainwater management and photovoltaic generation. Husbandry clauses provide a potential legal basis for setting out and enforcing the responsibilities that all stewards have to care for their land.

As in an ownership economy, the main purpose of such clauses is the positive one of promoting this care of the land. But prohibitions are also important, for example relating to the disposal of waste and the avoidance of pollution.

Damage on a single site

In a stewardship economy damage is assessed by means of regular inspection and revaluation of the 'disimprovement value' by the

Land Stewardship Authority. There are two possible approaches to assessing this value. The 'damage cost approach' assesses the actual damage caused. This is equal to the capitalisation of the expected loss of future stewardship fees for the site as the result of, for example, increased costs, reduced productivity, restrictions on its future use of insurance against health claims. Alternatively, the 'avoidance (or maintenance) cost approach' estimates the cost of measures that are required to reduce pollution to a given standard or otherwise return the site to its previous condition.

The estimation of the cost of disimprovements is not easy or free from subjective judgements. If pollution results in a health risk to people using the land, to take just one example, the value of the disimprovement will depend on the price put on people's health and life. And it may be difficult to assign a probability to a risk. However, the fact that such choices are placed at the centre of the tax system rather than being considered a purely social issue can only help to bring greater balance into the way we treat the natural world.

The collection of disimprovement values where a site has been damaged is a form of recompense to future generations for the destruction of natural capital. As explained in the previous chapter, this revenue must be invested in some other form of capital for their benefit, not distributed to those currently alive as Environmental Dividend.

Impact on neighbouring sites

Stewardship provides a straightforward universal mechanism for preventing people from shifting (externalising) the costs of pollution onto their neighbours. When a site suffers damage the steward has the duty to inform the stewardship authority, who inspect and quantify the disimprovement. If the pollution arises elsewhere the polluter has to pay the disimprovement value.

Issues of liability are determined by a tribunal of the Land Stewardship Trust. In view of the international nature of some pollution events there needs to be an international structure, although many disputes could be settled at a national or even local level.

How much pollution?

When a pollutant is discharged (emitted or dumped) into a sink, the amount discharged each year is a flow of pollutant. This flow adds to the stock of pollutant in the sink.

If a Stewardship Trust is to set limits to discharges, whether the pollution affects a single site, a neighbouring site or the whole world, it is essential to decide the optimal level (stock) of pollution and the acceptable limit to discharges (flows). There is no 'scientific' answer as the optimal level of pollution cannot be determined solely by means of a technical model. An accurate technical model is critically important, but what is also needed is a way of describing the trade-offs between the costs and benefits of pollution reduction (abatement). This requires a mechanism to aggregate across quite different sorts of thing – for example air pollution may give rise to loss of life, sickness and damage to buildings as well as to the additional costs of health care, clean-up and reduced visibility. It also requires a mechanism for aggregating across time, as the costs of abatement are felt now while the benefits are experienced after a time delay that may be substantial. This means that a Stewardship Trust needs an economic model if it is to identify the optimal level of pollution.

Discounting the future

Stewardship is compatible with any rate of discounting, though its emphasis on fairness and its acceptance that property rights are not perpetual or conditional should continually raise the issue of the discount rate and favour the long view. A green version of stewardship would choose a very low or zero rate of discounting while other versions might use the Government Green Book approach.

Chapter 9   Climate change

This chapter discusses an example of pollution that has a global impact – greenhouse gas emissions. There are many ways in which a stewardship economy is less prone to emit greenhouse gases than an ownership economy. It provides everyone with a fair share of the output of a complex economy and so does not need the economic growth that ownership economies rely on to provide jobs and tackle poverty. By making land more readily available for housing and business it can lead to more compact habitations and reduce the need for commuting. A stewardship economy reduces taxes on labour and so allows a shift in the balance of inputs to production, for example, from fossil fuels to labour in agriculture.

In a stewardship economy those emitting greenhouse gases need to pay, either by purchasing tradable emissions permits for each tonne of greenhouse gases emitted or by paying a carbon tax. The price mechanism has the potential to set limits to climate change and to shape individual behaviour.

A stewardship economy also provides people with ways to adapt to the change in our climate that is already inevitable, ensuring that it is not the poorest people who bear the whole of the burden.

Ownership economy

Our response to climate change

The increasingly detailed understanding and quantification of what climate change will mean for us, and the ever-narrowing confidence limits to these projections, have been documented in the reports of the International Panel on Climate Change (IPCC) since 1990. By 2006 they had concluded that there is a more than 90 per cent probability that the global warming observed over the last 50 years is the result of human activity. These reports may even underestimate the probability of the risk as they represent the consensus view of government scientists on whom political pressure may be brought to bear by governments who find it inconvenient to acknowledge the science.

There are many possible positive feedback mechanisms that could lead to severe and even runaway climate change. These include, for example, reduced uptake of CO2 as higher temperatures lead to plant death; release of CO2 by increasingly active soil micro-organisms; and release of methane from permafrost and the seabed. There may also be slowing and reversal of the Gulf Stream and severe rises in sea levels due to melting of the Greenland ice cap. Looking back at the 2000 report, even its worst predictions of CO2 levels in 2007 proved to be unduly optimistic.

Jared Diamond describes how several localised but long-established societies collapsed. These included Easter Island and the Maya,. He has identified a set of factors that together have influenced whether societies survive or collapse (Jared Diamond 2005:11). Friendly trade partners and hostile neighbours play important roles. Environmental damage or changes in climate are often critically important. One of the major differences between societies that survive and those that collapse is the way that they respond, or more commonly fail to respond, to environmental challenges.

The proximate cause of our profligate use of the atmosphere is that we have treated it as an open access regime, a sink into which everyone has been more or less free to discharge pollutants. Since the Kyoto Protocol in 1997 one tentative response has taken the potentially promising form of 'cap and trade', which introduces private property rights in the form of tradable emissions permits. However, these permits have largely been gifted to existing polluters ('grandfathered'), conferring profits on the polluters and costs on consumers). These gifts continue year on year, although fortunately they are reducing and the permits do not provide perpetual rights to pollute.

Mitigating climate change

Governments have tried a range of approaches to reducing (abating) the emissions of greenhouse gases, and so mitigating climate change. They have placed their faith in consumer choice, for example requiring manufacturers to label electrical appliances to show their energy consumption. In addition, they have taken a regulatory approach, for example, extending the building regulations to include standards of insulation. And they have made use of the price mechanism, for example increasing taxes on petrol and diesel while reducing taxes on vehicles that are energy efficient. All these approaches need to continue.

102

There is widespread consensus that a critically important component of any approach is to ensure that the price of goods, services and production process that emit greenhouse gases reflect their true cost, including all the costs of their contribution to climate change. This can be achieved either by annual auctions of permits to release greenhouse gases, or by imposing a tax.

The United Nations Framework Convention on Climate Change (UNFCCC) was adopted at the Rio Earth Summit in 1992. It provides a way for countries to work together to limit global temperature increases and climate change, and to cope with their impacts. It meets each year and several of these meetings have led to significant agreements – particularly in Kyoto, Doha and Paris.

Kyoto Protocol (2005 - 2012)

The Kyoto Protocol (1997) was the first international agreement to attempt to tackle climate change. It stipulated legally binding emission reduction targets for industrialised nations, and non-binding targets for non-industrialised nations. It did not specify how they should meet their commitments.

Its deficiencies are well rehearsed:

- the obligations fell only on 'developed' (high-consumption) economies, and so did not affect China and India

- many countries did not ratify the protocol, notably the USA.

- it covered only one greenhouse gas, CO_2

- it excluded international aviation (the responsibility of the International Civil Aviation Organisation) and shipping (the International Maritime Organisation)

- its relatively modest targets fell far short of what most people believed to be needed

- even the targets for 2008 to 2012 were missed by many signatories.

In spite of the fact that its recommendations were timid, it was a major diplomatic achievement to agree any form of binding agreement.

Doha amendment (2013 - 2020)

Russia, Japan and New Zealand withdrew from participation in the Kyoto Protocol. at the end of 2012. The Doha amendment (2012) covers just 38 countries (28 of which are in the EU) and just 14% of global emissions. These countries committed themselves to reducing emissions to at least 18% below 1990 levels. More than 70 countries made non-binding commitments.

Paris agreement (2016 -)

The Paris agreement (2016) contains an astonishingly ambitious long-term goal – to keep the global average temperature to well below 2°C above pre-industrial levels, and to pursue efforts to limit it to 1.5°C (a level that has probably already been reached).

Rather than reaching any international agreement about who would take what action, it hands the entire responsibility over to individual states. Many of these have undertaken to submit a national climate action plan every five years and have volunteered to adhere to their own Intended Nationally Determined Contribution (INDC). High consumption economies also agreed to continue to provide development aid to low consumption economies to enable them to reduce emissions and build resilience to the consequences of climate change.

Unilateral and multilateral commitments

Given this aspirational but unenforceable international agreement, the future of the Earth depends on the good intentions of individual states.

The European Union has been a leader in climate change agreements and action, and its Emissions Trading Scheme (EU ETS) was the first multilateral action taken to reduce CO_2 emissions. The scheme is described elsewhere, with a critique of the detail of its design. The European Union agreed to reduce greenhouse gas emissions by at least 40 per cent (from 1990 levels) by 2030 (2030 Climate and Energy Framework). The UK set a legally binding target of cutting emissions by 34 per cent by 2020 and 80 per cent by 2050 (Climate Change Act 2008). China unilaterally introduced legally binding curbs on greenhouse emissions. The American administration in 2017 does not believe in anthropogenic climate change and is unlikely to support the efforts of other countries.

There are many barriers to achieving greenhouse gas abatement. One is the commercial interests of the fossil fuel industries and their ability to lobby for favourable terms from governments. Another is the need for each country to remain economically competitive in its international trade. It is electoral readiness, political will and the enlightened self-interest of households and communities that will determine whether we take effective action to tackle climate change, not the availability of scientific understanding or economic mechanisms.

Adaptation to climate change

Even if we experience runaway climate change due to one or more positive feedback loops, some form of life is likely to continue on earth. But climate change is going to have serious impacts on many species, including our own. We are going to have to cope with, and adapt to, climate change.

The countries that are least able to adapt to climate change are the poorest countries. The people who are most vulnerable are the poorest members of society, as they live on the most vulnerable land. There are likely to be large numbers of 'environmental refugees'. Wealthier countries, and wealthier individuals within countries, will need to accommodate others to find new homes and new work.

Climate change will produce changes in land values. Some areas such as Greenland, Russia and Northern Europe can be expected to become more valuable as agricultural production rises and heating costs fall – though this may be an unduly optimistic scenario if environmental impacts elsewhere lead to global economic depression or if there are unexpected climate changes such as a reversal of the Gulf Stream.

Many areas including India and Africa are likely to experience drought, flooding and extreme climate events such as hurricanes. These events will mean that some areas become less productive and more expensive to insure, and land values will fall in these areas.

Most dramatic will be the areas of land that are lost to the sea, where land values will fall to zero. The IPCC report (2007? Compare with Stern) suggests that sea levels may rise by between

18 and 59 centimetres as a result of thermal expansion alone. If there is significant melting of the Greenland ice sheet, as already seems to be happening, the possible 7 metre rise in sea levels would destroy the Netherlands, the Maldives, Bangladesh and many coastal cities including London. Even a one metre rise in sea level will flood 17 per cent of Bangladesh. New Orleans provides a vivid example of a city that, following Hurricane Katrina in 2005, has shrunk to half its former population and has effectively accepted the need to abandon some areas for the rest of the city to survive.

To recap:

Climate change threatens to provoke mass migrations, territorial conflict, drought and increased social injustice as well as potentially irreversible damage to other species and to the global ecosystem. Ownership economies are driven to exacerbate climate change by their need to foster economic growth to reduce unemployment, poverty, inefficient land use and inequalities in wealth.

The most promising way for governments to tackle climate change is to put a price on the use of the atmosphere so that any goods or services that release greenhouse gases enter the market with a price that reflects their true cost, including the environmental damage caused in their production.

Stewardship economy

Stewardship offers a coherent approach to greenhouse gas emissions, based on the underlying principles that prices of goods and services should reflect their true cost; and that those who make use of more than their fair (equal) share of the natural world need to compensate those who use less than their share.

Consequences of a stewardship economy

A stewardship economy contains mechanisms, described below, for mitigating climate change by putting a realistic price on the emission of greenhouse gases and for adapting to climate change by sharing the burden of costs when land becomes uninhabitable. But just as important are the many ways in which a stewardship economy places much less of a burden on the environment, even when the level of economic activity is unchanged. These include the more efficient use of land, the substitution of satisfying work for the use of fossil fuels and the lack of need for economic growth.

Efficient use of land

Land, in a stewardship economy, ceases to have any value as an investment and there is always a pressure to put it to use. Land that is, in an ownership economy, underused and derelict becomes available for housing and business and the cost of using land falls. People are no longer forced to commute long distances to work and there is much more co-location of housing and work, compact settlements, reduced commuting and reduced emissions from transport.

Labour-intensive enterprises

In an ownership economy taxes make labour expensive (National Insurance Contributions, Income Tax). This would be turned on its head in a stewardship economy. Agriculture, for example, would cease to be today's isolated and lonely work in a depopulated countryside as farmers were able to employ more workers, opportunities opened up for smallholding and more people chose to work in a healthy outdoor environment.

Abandon economic growth

In an ownership economy the bulk of the product of our complex economy finds its way into the hands of the owners of monopoly rights – particularly rights to land and intellectual property – with a small minimum being paid to the providers of labour and capital. The only way for most people to participate in the economy is through work or the receipt of benefits, and the income from either of these is generally inadequate to support a satisfying life. So, for most people the only hope, particularly when jobs are difficult to find, is the promise of trickle-down from a growing economy.

In a stewardship economy the product is shared out as a Universal Income. The rent of the whole country is channelled, after deducting the necessary expenses of government, into equal shares for everyone. The availability of land for work, the receipt of the Universal Income and the disappearance of rentier income lead to a society much more equal in income and wealth. The pressures on individuals to take on unsatisfying work and the pressures on government to reduce unemployment disappear. The existential need for economic growth melts away and fossil fuel consumption falls.

Mitigating climate change

In a stewardship economy there is a regulatory body and a stewardship trust that hold in trust the property rights to the atmosphere, just as there is a trust for the land and other aspects of the environment. For consistency this might be called the Atmosphere Stewardship Trust, but Peter Barnes has already proposed a global body with this function that has the more appealing name 'Sky Trust' (Peter Barnes, 2001). This section uses his name for it even though he envisages this commons trust as combining the roles of regulator and stewardship trust.

Sky Trust

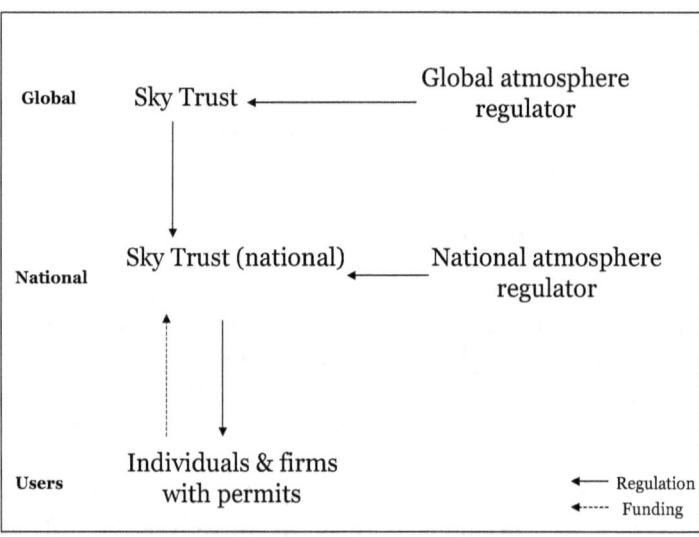

The national Sky Trust might be constituted in a variety of ways. Socialists might like it to be a government department. Liberals might like it to be a social enterprise or 'not-for-profit' company. Libertarians would probably favour a private sector business, which would be awarded the right to operate as the Stewardship Trust through a bidding process that would capture most of the market rent of the resource. This mechanism would, as with the national lottery now, allow the incumbent to be displaced by a rival bidder when its franchise came to an end.

Institutional response - acting in time

In an established stewardship economy we would already have had in place the economic instruments and institutions to tackle greenhouse gas emissions. We would have recognised the dangers of open access regimes for resources like the atmosphere. We would have responded to the 19th century challenge of particulate pollution from coal burning in cities not just by enacting the Clean Air Acts but by setting up a Sky Trust to manage atmospheric pollution of all sorts. This body might have recognised, and responded to, the harm caused by particulates emitted by diesel engines. It would surely have recognised and acted on the threat of climate change much earlier, and it would certainly have been held accountable if it had responded as slowly as we have.

We can only speculate whether, if a stewardship economy had existed over the last half a century, the sense that we are all stewards not owners of the natural world would have led us to take action as soon as the case for climate change had been made on the balance of probabilities, rather than waiting until it was beyond (un)reasonable doubt. This ability to make an early response to future environmental challenges would be a major advantage of a stewardship economy.

Regulation

The first step toward stewardship is for the regulator to establish the extent of the property to which there will be property rights. For land this requires mapping, for greenhouse gases it means establishing the capacity of the atmosphere to act as a sink. In an ideal world this is carried out by a global, or at least international, regulatory body which decides a sustainable global rate of greenhouse gas emissions. Each country is allocated its share of this 'global carbon budget' in proportion to the size of its population – so each individual has an equal share and each country has an annual 'national carbon budget'. If there is no such international agreement, a national atmosphere regulator acting responsibly should decide a national rate of greenhouse gas emissions that is the equal to what would have been agreed if there had been an international agreement.

Behavioural change

Once the national carbon budget has been decided, the national Sky Trust is responsible for ensuring that it is not exceeded.

The behaviour changes that we will all need to make if we are to reduce our emissions of greenhouse gases will be the same in stewardship and ownership economies. We will need, amongst other things, to insulate our homes, travel by public transport and energy-efficient vehicles, generate electricity in ways that do not release CO_2 into the atmosphere, abandon our reliance on air travel, move towards a vegan diet, change the nature of agricultural production, implement sequestration of CO_2 and methane, develop an alternative to cement and dramatically reduce our dependence on products that are in any way responsible for releasing greenhouse gases.

The Sky Trust will need to make use of regulations, taxes and subsidies to support these changes. But it will rely to a great extent on the way that individuals respond to true cost pricing. The true cost price could be established by accurately setting a carbon tax but is most likely to be set by auctioning tradable permits for greenhouse gases as well as removing existing subsidies for fossil fuels.

Removing subsidies

The most damaging and expensive subsidies currently apply to energy. Existing fuel subsidies lower the cost of carbon, and they need to be removed if the price of fuel is to reflect its true cost. Examples include the low rate of tax on diesel for agricultural use and the exclusion from taxation in the aviation and shipping industries, resulting in subsidised long-distance trade.

Tradable emissions permits

If stewardship is implemented on a national scale tradable permits would be issued equal to the national carbon budget and allocated in such a way that everyone in the country benefits equally. If stewardship is implemented on a global scale the revenue derived from allocating the global carbon budget is divided equally amongst everyone on the planet. The overall impact is that anyone who uses more than their fair (equal) share compensates those who use less than their share. The simplest way to divide the budget is for organisations that emit carbon to buy permits, which are sold at an annual auction.

An alternative approach, also fully compatible with stewardship, is the use of Personal Carbon Allowances such as Tradable Energy Quotas. These have the same impact on energy use and the distribution of wealth as permit auctions and the Environmental Dividend. They are more cumbersome to administer but have the great advantage of making everyone aware of their carbon footprint and their responsibility to minimise it.

Transition

Since the early 1990s the Global Commons Institute has proposed that the global carbon budget should 'contract' and that national carbon budgets should 'converge'. Convergence means that the national carbon budgets should initially reflect the current national rates of emissions but that these should converge towards equal per capita emissions on a date to be negotiated. Bearing in mind the historical emissions of high-consumption economies, this proposal for convergence is very generous to these economies. 'Contract and converge' would be the most appropriate way to manage transition in the allocation of permits in a stewardship economy.

We should treat the atmosphere as a non-renewable resource and invest its resource rent for the benefit of future generations to develop carbon-neutral alternatives and to adapt to climate change. However, during transition, which for greenhouse gas emissions may need to be prolonged, it is more important that a true cost price is established than that the revenue is spent in an ideal way. For this reason, the revenue should be distributed on an equal per capita basis as an Environmental Dividend.

Adaptation to climate change

Climate change will cause hardship in a stewardship economy just as it will in an ownership economy. There will be famines, floods and droughts, and there will be damage and loss of buildings and improvements. But the burden will be shared more equally. When land values fall or disappear the loss is borne by everyone. Suppose that land is flooded and its steward moves away. They lose their buildings and improvements but suffer no financial loss from the destruction of land value. We all lose the part of the Universal Income that would have come from that land. In this way some of the localised cost of climate change is shared out amongst everyone, and those who need to relocate are supported in the transition by their Universal Income.

Another feature of stewardship is that if a government decides that it would be prudent to take steps to adapt to climate change, for example to minimise flooding by strengthening flood defences, there is an obvious source of revenue – the stewardship fees paid by the properties that they protect.

See Stewardship Economy: Book 2 for the practical proposals for how stewardship can mitigate climate change.

Chapter 10   Energy

This chapter considers the question: How does stewardship influence the availability and consumption of energy?

Physics and economics of energy production

All economies maintain their complexity – their low entropy – by consuming energy. The extraction and consumption of this energy, and its conversion from one form to another, has environmental and human as well as financial costs.

Net energy ratio

Underlying any economic considerations is the physical reality of energy production, and in particular the net energy ratio of fuels – the ratio of the amount of energy provided by a fuel to the amount of energy expended in extracting or producing it. Just as it doesn't make nutritional sense for a subsistence farmer to expend more calories growing food than they get from the food itself, there is not a lot to be gained from producing fuel with a net energy ratio of less than one. The only exception is when this fuel is more effective – for example because it has high energy density or is a useful energy store. The prime example of this is hydrogen as a fuel for transport.

Energy efficiency

One obvious way to reduce the cost of energy is to make better use of it by increasing the efficiency with which it is used – particularly for domestic use (space heating, water heating and appliances), transport, commercial and industrial purposes.

Demand management

Although energy efficiency is part of the solution, it is not enough on its own. Reducing the cost of energy generally leads to a compensatory increase in demand – people drive further or faster or turn up the thermostat. So, energy efficiency measures need to be combined with an increase in the cost of energy to damp down demand. The problem with measures that increase energy costs is that, in ownership economies, they bear most heavily on the poor.

Regulation

Regulation is needed where prices alone will not produce the necessary changes in behaviour. Examples include:

- planning and building regulations

- energy efficiency standards for domestic appliances, including proscribing unnecessary standby functions

- speed limits on the roads

- requirements to provide information such as:

- carbon footprint of food and other goods

- smart electricity and gas meters to provide a continuous display of greenhouse gas emissions.

Subsidies

Across the world in 2014 governments spent $550 billion subsidising the production and consumption of fossil fuels (Economist 17/1/15: 9). There are also substantial subsidies for nuclear power, renewables and biofuels (which are widely misused). We need prices that reflect the true cost of carbon and other pollutants, whether this is achieved by means of a carbon tax or by auctioning tradable permits.

Ownership economy

Affordability

Although it is the rich who have heated swimming pools, sports utility vehicles and frequent international flights it is the poor who spend a greater proportion of their income on energy. This is partly because the poor inevitably spend more of their income on basic necessities like keeping warm, while the rich have more 'discretionary' spending and are able to save more. But an important contributing factor is the standard of insulation in their homes, particularly in the rented sector where the tenant pays the heating bills, and the landlord has no financial incentive to invest in energy-efficiency.

Energy use by the poor has been subsidised, at the request of the regulator, through the application of cheaper tariffs for 'social users' and those who use small amounts – though these groups have also been exploited by higher charges for the use of pre-payment meters rather than payment by direct debit. It is because of this impact on the poorest that VAT has been held at a low level on domestic fuels – exactly the opposite of what is needed to reduce carbon emissions.

Non-renewables

Fossil fuels

Oil plays such an important role in our economy because it combines a high net energy ratio with a high energy density, making it particularly suitable for transport applications.

It's always hazardous to predict the imminent exhaustion of natural resources. But Richard Heinberg (Richard Heinberg 2003) placed contemporary society near the middle of a period of history he calls the 'Petroleum Interval', which began with the drilling of the first commercial oil well in Pennsylvania in 1859. During the first half of the Petroleum Interval demand for oil has increased dramatically. But, in spite of the limitations to supplies caused by wars and the OPEC cartel, it has generally been a buyers' market. This will change as the peak of extraction is passed.

The current best estimate for the peak in global production lies between 2006 and 2015. Although oil reserves are ultimately determined by geological factors, the amount actually extracted will depend not only on the size of the reserves but on price, technology and infrastructure factors. Rising prices will reduce demand, stimulate energy conservation and efficiency in use, increase exploratory effort and efficiency of recovery, and stimulate the development of substitutes including shale oil and oil sand. But this may not be enough to make a significant difference because of the physical constraint that underlies energy extraction – the amount of energy input that it takes to extract a unit of energy. The net energy ratio of an energy source must be greater than 1 if that source is to be worth extracting. The net energy ratio of oil has fallen from over 100 for oil extracted in the 1940s to 8 for oil fields discovered in the 1970s, while the ratio for shale oil lies between 13 and 0.7.

Coal is abundant but in addition to releasing carbon dioxide it is responsible for particulate pollution and the sulphur dioxide that is the main cause of acid rain. Coal's net energy ratio is 30 for direct heating and 9 for electricity production (2.5 where scrubbers are used). The net energy ratio is falling over the years as less productive mines are be developed, and the net energy ratio for electricity generation has been predicted to fall to 1 by 2040. If this happens, it will no longer be worth producing coal for this purpose.

Unless demand falls, which seems highly unlikely given the growing economies of large countries like China and India, oil will become more expensive as it becomes more scarce. The economic, social and military impact is difficult to imagine.

Nuclear power

In principle, nuclear fission could be a renewable source of energy, though most current reactors require a source of uranium. Reserves are thought to be adequate in the medium term. But the environmental and social costs of nuclear power, like those of fossil fuels, have been ignored and this has led to excessive investment in nuclear power.

The cost of extraction of nuclear fuel includes the release of greenhouse gases, the health costs of exposure to radioactive isotopes and contamination of the site.

The costs of generation include the safe operation and decommissioning of the reactor, the safe disposal of all radioactive components and the supervision of the waste till the radioactivity has decayed.

An additional risk of nuclear power is that fuel, or indeed waste, may be used by independent or state terrorists. This is not limited to the high technology of nuclear weapons development and may include spreading nuclear contamination, for example in a 'dirty bomb' using conventional explosives; or a terrorist may launch an attack on nuclear facilities. These risks mean that all stages of the nuclear fuel cycle need to be subjected to independent inspection to verify that radioactive material, including waste, is not being diverted; and that nuclear facilities, including fuel in transport, need to be guarded against attack and theft. The full costs of inspection and security are currently externalised by the nuclear power industry and passed on to the state.

In both the United States and the United Kingdom, operators of nuclear power stations have only very limited liability for major incidents. Governments bear the unquantified risk of insuring them.

Renewables

Electricity generation

In the UK, electricity production by solar power increased rapidly from 2010 as a result of government subsidy to the feed-in tariff and - as this government subsidy reduced - the falling cost of photovoltaic (PV) panels. The cumulative installed capacity of solar photovoltaics rose from 95 megawatts in 2010 to 13,563 megawatts by the end of 2020.

https://www.google.com/search?q=electricity+from+pv+panels+uk+2010+to+2020&rlz=1C1CHBF_en-GBGB908GB908&oq=electricity+from+pv+panels+uk+2010+to+2020&aqs=chrome..69i57.19544j0j4&sourceid=chrome&ie=UTF-8

However, there have been concerns about the environmental impact of manufacture of solar photovoltaic panels, but many studies have shown that they pay for themselves in carbon reductions and embodied energy and electricity in a short period (one to six years), which is good news given that they can be expected to function for 25 years.in carbon reductions, embodied energy and electricity, all redeemed well within their operational lifecycle. In addition, as more photovoltaic units are made, the carbon cost per unit is reduced further reducing the carbon and energy 'payback' period.

https://www.renewableenergyhub.co.uk/main/solar-panels/solar-panels-carbon-analysis/

Biofuels

Biofuels offer a renewable source of energy that may be produced close to where it is used, reducing transport costs and contributing to fuel security. The consumption of biofuels releases greenhouse gases, but their production process may remove greenhouse gases from the atmosphere. They are becoming more economically attractive as the costs of fossil fuels rise.

Biofuels require the consumption of fossil fuels for harvesting, processing and in the production of fertilisers. Some biofuel crops, like oil seed rape and sugar cane, are grown in competition with food crops and so raise food prices. Twenty five per cent of America's corn is converted to ethanol. Some palm oil plantations have been created by clearing rainforest, which means that their impact on climate change is harmful.

Other biofuels, such as coconut husks, and bagasse, a fibrous residue from sugar cane, use the waste products of food production and so potentially lower food costs, while jatropha plantations regenerate dry and eroded soils.

Hydrogen

Liquid hydrogen has a high energy density, which makes it attractive for transport applications and the most practical alternative to oil as a fuel for aircraft. It is essentially a mechanism to store energy, like a battery and has a net energy ratio of less than one.

Stewardship economy

Subsidies

There may be a limited place for subsidies where regulation and true cost pricing do not have the desired effect, but there is absolutely no justification for subsidising fossil fuels, nuclear power or indeed any established technology.

True cost pricing

The main role of government in managing energy use in a stewardship economy is to ensure that energy prices reflect the true cost to the environment of its production and use.

All land that is used for energy production including generation, extraction, refining and storage attract stewardship fees. These fees, along with the cost of emissions permits for CO_2 and the full costs of insurance, ensure that the price of all electricity that is generated reflects its true cost. This feeds through into higher prices of many products as businesses are prevented from shifting onto others the cost of their damage to the environment.

Affordability

A key feature of stewardship is that all the revenue derived from the auction of permits for renewable resources is distributed on an equal per capita basis as an Environmental Dividend. For pragmatic reasons fossil fuels, even though they are clearly not renewable, should for the time being probably be treated in the same way but eventually this revenue stream will need to be invested for future generations.

Regulation

Regulatory interventions, such as those relating to fuel efficient appliances and insulation of homes, play their part in a stewardship economy just as they do in an ownership economy. They become less important as prices reflect true costs.

Non-renewables

Fossil fuels

How might the Petroleum Interval have played out if stewardship had been in place at the outset? In recognition that oil reserves are finite, would we have invested the revenue from their extraction in human and physical capital for the benefit of future generations instead of using them to finance current consumption? Would we have taken the difficult decision to deliberately reduce the rate of extraction at particular oil and coal fields by issuing and auctioning extraction permits? There is no knowing. If we had done so we would not have depleted our natural capital so rapidly and would have delayed reaching Peak Oil. We would have fortuitously contributed less to climate change, though as a result the evidence for anthropogenic climate change would have been less compelling and might have been ignored for even longer than it has been.

What we can be sure is that the price of fossil fuels are higher in a stewardship economy than in an ownership economy as the costs of carbon permits are included in their price and are passed on to consumers, including firms that produce goods and services, as a true cost price. This reduces demand for these products.

Electricity generating plants would have to pay stewardship fees for the generation site as well as the true cost price of the raw material.

Nuclear power

Stewardship requires the price of nuclear-generated electricity to reflect its true human and environmental costs. The costs incurred by the nuclear industry would include insurance, paid to a credible independent insurer with unlimited liability, that would enable full payment to be made for any adverse consequences at any time in the future – including those resulting from terrorist activity. Most significantly this would include the costs to human health, environmental damage caused by all stages of the nuclear fuel cycle, the projected costs of decommissioning and waste management, and the necessary security measures as well as the usual operating costs. In the case of an incident like Chenobyl, for example, this includes the ongoing cost of lost stewardship fees from the area that has to be evacuated as well as the value of the buildings and other improvements.

Most countries have concluded that the best form of disposal of nuclear waste is in deep, stable rock formations where the waste is unlikely to contaminate the water table or be disturbed by seismic activity. Even when possible sites have been identified, it is likely that local people will still oppose that disposal unless they have already had significant exposure to the nuclear industry. In the UK the Committee on Radioactive Waste Management proposed that local authorities should be allowed to bid for a subsidy that would be paid by the national government if disposal goes ahead at that site. This quantifies the impact of the development and helps people to see that they are being compensated. Stewardship provides this sort of compensation automatically, without the need for a specific subsidy, as the proximity of the dump reduces the desirability of land, its price and therefore the stewardship fees that local people have to pay.

The decision about whether to build new nuclear plants in a stewardship economy will depend on a cost-benefit analysis that takes into account all these factors. The most contentious issue will be the discount rate which will need to take into account the fact that the costs of nuclear power may stretch on for thousands or even millions of years. Greens will favour a discount rate of close to zero, while others discount future consequences more highly, probably at the real interest rate.

There may be no greater likelihood of agreement about the discount rate in a stewardship economy than in an ownership economy, but it is possible that if people really internalise their role as steward of the planet they may be less likely to discount the future and so to tolerate costs that extend far into the future.

120

Renewables

Electricity generation

In a stewardship economy all electricity generation including renewables like hydro, wind, solar, wave, tidal and geothermal have to pay stewardship fees for the generating site; though the value of the land is likely to be reduced by the planning permission that will have been granted for the construction of the plant. They also have to pay any disimprovement value they create; for example, for land flooded by dams, loss of amenity value from noise and views, or damage to wildlife habitats. A stewardship economy tips the balance in favour of electricity generation from renewables because the costs of fossil fuels and nuclear power are much higher in a stewardship economy.

Micro-generation

When electricity is generated on the roofs or within homes or public buildings there are no stewardship fees to pay for the generation site. And micro-generation does not suffer from transmission losses, which are more costly when electricity prices are higher in a stewardship economy. This approach becomes even more attractive with technological development. Micro-generation of electricity is encouraged, whether this is from domestic combined heat and power plants, solar panels or domestic wind turbines.

Biofuels

The cost of production of a biofuel will include the stewardship fees of the land on which the crops are grown – which will be higher where there is more competition for the use of land for fuel and for food. There will be costs for fertiliser and water and it will be important to ensure that disimprovements like the loss of biodiversity, hedgerows and wildlife are accounted for. All these costs, which are shifted onto others (externalised) in ownership economies are included in the price of the fuel in a stewardship economy – true cost pricing.

In a stewardship economy electricity generated from fossil fuels will be more expensive, largely because its price reflects the true cost of the environmental impact of greenhouse gases. Energy efficiency measures, and energy generated by renewable means, are in principle, more likely to be developed and adopted due to the high cost of electricity generated from fossil fuels. However, the price of nuclear power, too, reflects its true costs and this will put economic limits on whether there is investment in new nuclear plant.

Chapter 11   Measures to encourage sustainability

Land has been held as private property for millennia, and some aspects of the environment such as oil and mineral rights have also been privately held. Other important aspects of the environment have been held as open access regimes (for example the atmosphere and the oceans), as common-pool resources (for example fisheries, lakes) or collectively (for example landfill sites).

As we have attempted to reduced environmental destruction, the main approach has been to bring open access regimes into some form of property rights. The debate has been about the merits and demerits of private, collective and common rights. Stewardship offers a form of property right that is more suited to the protecting environment – a use-right that is not perpetual but conditional on payment of fees or charges.

What is the most effective way to encourage people and businesses to care for land and the environment? Many non-economic factors influence people including altruism, tradition and social pressures. Governments may reinforce or undermine these through the allocation of property rights and through economic mechanisms like subsidies, regulation and taxes. This chapter explores the advantages and disadvantages of these approaches.

Ownership economy

We have demonstrated that it is possible to tackle global environmental issues in many different ways:

Chlorofluorocarbons (CFCs) were extensively used in refrigerants and aerosol propellants and were shown to be creating a hole in the ozone layer. A **regulatory** approach, the Montreal protocol, has resulted in an 80 per cent reduction in their production .

While the European Union successfully tackled sulphur dioxide (SO2) emissions, a major cause of acid rain, by regulatory means, the USA instituted a regime based on a form of **property rights**, tradable permits, that has resulted in a 50 per cent reduction in its emission). The price of permits fell as the cost of reducing emissions (abatement) has fallen.

Taxes on vehicle fuel have stimulated the design and production of more fuel-efficient vehicles.

Subsidies have stimulated the installation of both domestic insulation in the UK and photovoltaic panels in Germany.

The implementation challenge lies as much in whether these approaches can be made acceptable to electorates as in their effectiveness.

The most serious examples of pollution occur where there are no property rights, and pollutants are discharged into a sink that is managed as an open access regime. Collective property is more vulnerable than private property because the property rights are weaker and more impersonal. If some aspect of the environment is held as private or common property the owner has an incentive, however imperfect, to look after and maintain the value of the property. They may also have legal recourse against others who damage it.

However, collective (state) action, governance by groups of commoners and market-based solutions have all proved capable of reducing at least some forms of environmental damage.

Collective action – regulation

Requiring good practice

When there are clear uncontested examples of good environmental practice the government can play an important leadership role by insisting that these are adopted.

Building standards were introduced in the UK in the 19th century in response to the well-publicised collapse of a number of poorly built houses. These regulations provide buyers with an assurance that certain minimum standards have been met and improve the efficiency of the land market by ensuring that information is available. They assist conscientious builders who want to meet these standards but would find themselves unable to compete with firms that build to lower standards.

New energy-efficient buildings have substantially lower running costs than traditional buildings. When the insulation is included in the design it adds only a few percent to the construction costs. Adding this level of insulation to an existing building is much more expensive, so there are good reasons for this to be required by the building regulations. There need to be tighter insulation standards for all buildings, particularly when they are being refurbished, not just new ones.

On an industrial scale, pollution in the European Union is generally managed by requiring firms to register with the regulatory body and to use the 'best practicable means' (BPM) of reducing emissions. Sometimes environmental regulation falls, appropriately, on individuals and families. Reducing the speed limit from 70 to 60 miles per hour n UK motorways would reduce overall reduce the overall CO2 emissions from road transport by 2%. https://publications.parliament.uk/pa/cm200506/cmselect/cmenvaud/981/981we57.htm

Regulation can be relatively quick and straightforward to introduce and implement, requiring no more than legislation and policing. It may also feel much fairer than economic instruments as it applies equally to everyone, irrespective of their ability to pay. But regulations may be misguided and inflexible. Their origins may lie in lobbying by commercial interests or special interest groups intent on protecting their own position.

Spatial planning

Spatial planning is 'what can and should happen where' https://apps.caerphilly.gov.uk/LDP/Examination/PDF/W43-People-Places-Futures-The-Wales-Spatial-Plan.pdf

This is a regulatory approach which has a major impact on environmental issues and may be the only way to achieve the desired ends. Examples include restricting developments in green belt areas, permitting the development of renewable energy generation and allowing people to work close to their home in mixed developments.

Quotas

In 1988 a European Union directive successfully imposed a cap on sulphur dioxide emissions from existing large electricity generation plants, in addition to specifying the abatement technology to be used in new plants. And there have been successes even in the global or multi-national contexts that are the most challenging. The Montreal Protocol, which tackles the problem of depletion of the stratospheric ozone layer by chlorofluorocarbons (CFCs), provides an example by setting limits for each country on production of CFCs, with penalties for countries that violate the protocol.

Common property

Important aspects of the environment – particularly fisheries, forests, grazing and irrigation systems – have been managed by groups of commoners across the world and over the course of millennia. These are common-pool resources – resources that are large enough to make it costly (but not impossible) physically to exclude free-riders. Some examples have been successful, some unsuccessful. They are neither state nor market solutions, and their governance relies on self-organisation by the commoners.

Private property rights

Market mechanisms can, given some rather unlikely assumptions, give rise to an allocation of resources that is efficient in the sense of being Pareto optimal – no change could be made without disadvantaging someone. One of the assumptions is that there are well-defined property rights in everything of importance in the economy. Another is that people and firms bear the cost, and reap the reward, of what they do – that their costs and benefits are not 'externalised'.

True cost prices

Where the environment has been managed as an open access regime, there has been no price to pay for the damage done to it. This has led to overproduction and overconsumption because there is no penalty for us as individuals and firms for polluting and depleting natural resources, even though this is clearly unsustainable.

Economic approaches to managing the environment depend on making sure that everyone who uses the environment pays a price that reflects the true cost of the damage they cause to the environment – a true cost price. As mentioned above, this may be achieved through the application of taxes, tradable permits or legal liability. It would be possible to ensure that prices reflect the true costs of emissions, provided that taxes and charges (Pigouvian fees) are set equal to the marginal abatement cost – the cost of abating one more unit of pollution.

Taxes and charges

Taxes and charges for using the environment are levied in ownership economies, but their purpose has usually just been to provide funds for the management of the regulatory system, or for environmental clean-up operations. This is evident from the level at which they are set, which is far too low to provide an economic incentive to reduce (abate) discharges. Firms find that it is cheaper to pay the taxes and charges than cut emissions.

If taxes and charges levied by government are to achieve some intended reduction in emissions, it is necessary for the government to know how much this emissions abatement would actually cost a firm. When information is available about abatement costs, economic theory suggests that the choice between taxes and tradable permits depends on the relative slopes of the marginal damage and the marginal savings curves for emissions. When firms have significantly greater knowledge than the state, prices will be closer to the real marginal abatement cost if the state issues permits, and firms establish the price by bidding for permits in the market.

An optimal arrangement may be a combination of both permits and fees (or reimbursements) for firms that produce more (or less) than their permitted amounts.

The main advantages of taxes and charges is that, once the level has been set, they are easier to administer, and the price is less volatile than when permits are auctioned. The main disadvantages are the uncertainties about how firms will respond, whether they will achieve the desired level of abatement and the susceptibility of taxation to political manipulation.

Pragmatic considerations may be more important than the ideal prescribed by economic theory – the European Emissions Trading Scheme was successfully introduced in a situation where proposals for a new tax, requiring unanimity amongst member states, would have failed.

Tradable permits

When there are multiple users of some aspect of the environment, like the atmosphere as a sink for greenhouse gases, a national or international body may require all those who emit greenhouse gases to surrender permits to match their emissions. It has a regulatory function, deciding on the maximum amount of emissions that it wants to see in a year, the cap. And it has an executive function, making permits for this level of emissions available either by gift or by auction. It then needs to monitor emissions and to fine anyone for emissions for which they have not surrendered permits.

Tradable permits gained credibility when they were used in the USA in 1995 to reduce the emissions from power stations of sulphur dioxide – though Europe had equal success using a regulatory approach. The level at which sulphur dioxide emissions were capped was chosen - not as a result of rigorous cost-benefit analysis but - through political negotiations that took account of a good-enough interpretation of the science.

Economics and the environment

Non-commensurability

Some people argue that the costs and benefits of environmental damage are not commensurable, that they simply cannot be weighed against each other (Stuart McBurney 1990). But, in all areas of our lives, we make trade-offs between alternatives that are very different from each other. We recognise that these trade-offs are not ideal but least-worst. One way to aggregate and compare different sorts of costs and benefits across time is to use the currency of money.

Markets and profiteering

However, managing the environment by using the price mechanism opens it up to exploitation by business. No one who saw how financial firms inadvertently engineered the credit crunch in 2007 should be willing to trust that markets are naturally beneficial. Polluters have already profited from environmental pricing, for example by the grandfathering of carbon permits and some carbon offsetting schemes have bordered on the fraudulent. In spite of its deficiencies, the price mechanism has a great deal to offer.

128

Anthropocentric view

Economics privileges human values and priorities over those of other species. We should remain aware of this limitation and be ready to question the consequences of economic thinking whenever these conflict with the long-term interests of other species and the ecosystem as a whole.

Legal liability

Tort law provides legal remedies for wrongs that are inflicted in ways that are not criminal or covered by contracts. This provides a different way to ensure that potential polluters take account of (internalise) the costs that their pollution imposes on others (externalises).

It may be a useful approach, particularly where emissions are intermittent and unintended. Critically, it requires the existence of private property rights. For example, if the owner of land through which a stream passes has property rights over an unpolluted stream, they will be able to obtain redress over someone introducing pollution upstream.

Some arenas are covered by strict (no-fault) liability under tort law. This ensures that any polluter who damages the property of another person or firm is liable to pay compensation equal to the damage inflicted. Other arenas are governed by negligence liability, where the polluter is only liable if they fail to meet the 'legal standard of care'. Both forms of liability in theory cause potential polluters to adopt the same socially desirable, and economically efficient, level of precaution (Kolstad 2002:230)

Subsidies

If consumers and private enterprise are slow to adopt technology that the government judges to be beneficial to the environment, why not encourage them to do so by means of a subsidy?

Subsidies are often introduced in an attempt to remedy a failure of the price mechanism. If the price of electricity generated from fossil fuels is not a true cost price because it does not reflect the damage done by the greenhouse gases that it produces, it should be no surprise that people are slow to manufacture and purchase solar panels. There would, in theory, be no need for a subsidy if electricity were to be priced at its true cost.

Subsidies work by encouraging people who might change their behaviour by providing a financial incentive to do so. But they distort the price mechanism and its ability to shape both consumption and production; and produce 'unexpected' consequences. If a product or service is subsidised, more will be consumed than without the subsidy – subsidies for white bread discouraged people from eating healthier wholemeal bread and even encouraged its use as animal feed. One early consequence of generous subsidies for solar panels in Germany was to increase global demand so much that their price rose, and they became less affordable in sunnier countries where they would generate more electricity (Economist 17/3/07).

Subsidies appeal to politicians as they provide a way to favour industrial special interest groups. They are often a memorial to the power of lobbying and corruption.

Stewardship economy

Many of the mechanisms devised to manage the environment in ownership economies would be deployed in stewardship economies. Private property rights and the price mechanism would be widely used, along with regulation where appropriate. Where there is any threat to the environment, all open access regimes would be transferred into private or common property.

Collective action – regulation, subsidies and collective property

Regulation

It might seem that there is no need for regulation if the price of energy reflects its true costs. But there are problems where information is asymmetric. The buyer of a building may not know how energy-efficient it is (the information issue); landlords make investment decisions about buildings, but tenants pay the heating bills (the issue of agency); and people do not weigh future costs and benefits very highly, particularly people in poverty who tend to have the least energy-efficient homes (high discount rates).

In a similar way and for similar reasons there is a compelling case for the regulation of the environmental impact of a range of consumer products, just as there is for regulating their safety –

energy-efficient lightbulbs and domestic appliances, fuel-efficient lead-free cars with catalytic converters and so on.

The Montreal Protocol is an example of a regulation that produced a massive reduction in emissions of CFCs, leading to repair of the hole in the ozone layer a great an impact on mitigating climate change.(Economist 20/9/14: 26).

A stewardship economy would make some use of regulations that stipulate good practice, such as spatial planning which lies at the heart of the economy, public debate and political choice and is an essential element in stewardship of the environment.

Most regulations impose greater costs on end-users. But some reduce the longer-term costs to consumers by, for example, increasing the energy-efficiency of cars and homes. These regulatory interventions are not enough on their own because people respond by buying bigger cars, driving longer distances at greater speed or increasing the temperature of their homes. The lower costs of driving or of heating the home lead to an increase in demand for energy. Energy efficiency measures that make it possible to cut energy use need to be combined with true cost pricing that provides the incentive to do so.

Subsidies

Ensuring that goods and services carry a true cost price is generally a better form of government intervention than providing subsidies, which distort true cost pricing. If biofuels are subsidised, or indeed if there is a requirement for the use of a certain proportion of biofuels in road fuel, this may reduce demand for other sorts of energy. The price of other renewables may fall, reducing the incentive to develop hydroelectric and wind power.

But there are times where true cost pricing is not enough on its own and subsidies can be helpful. One example is where desirable activities have a long time-course – funding for research and development, for example, like the development of the technology for carbon capture. Research and development is always likely to need a subsidy, which may come either from government or from a charitable foundation.

Another example is where a new technology, like solar panels, may become much cheaper once it is being manufactured in large volumes. If you rely on true cost pricing to initiate development, the price of carbon might have to rise to unpalatably high levels before it was worth the risk of starting to produce the panels.

Yet another example is to combat the effect of the unequal distribution of wealth. 'Demand' in an economic sense is the wish to purchase goods or services that is backed by the ability to pay for them. Poor people are often unable to 'demand' things that they would very much like such as, for example, well-insulated homes. True cost pricing of energy falls more heavily on the poor. Subsidies for home insulation may play a key role in reducing greenhouse gas emissions in a relatively fair way as well as preventing vulnerable people from suffering. So, a stewardship economy will need to make judicious use of subsidies, while always asking whether its aims can be better met by market means.

Common property

The commons lie at the heart of a stewardship economy, and stewardship naturally lends itself to an approach in which the wealth of the natural world is held by Stewardship Trusts on behalf of all people. A Sky Trust or Atmosphere Stewardship Trust holds in trust common or collective property rights in air quality, a Watersheds Stewardship Trust holds common or collective property rights over rivers and streams, and so on.

These trusts may act using regulation or taxation but the most natural approach, and one that requires least reliance on the state, is to auction tradable permits.

Tradable permits

Stewardship Trusts auction permits that allow individuals or firms to use a defined amount of these resources during a defined period of time – use-rights – creating a form of private property rights.

We cannot assume, even if these permits are traded at a price in the market that reflects the marginal abatement cost, that the market will actually allocate emissions with perfect efficiency. But it a market in a stewardship economy would take greater note than at present of issues like pollution.

The advantages that permits have over both taxes and regulation include:

Information about abatement costs

If a regulator wants to limit emissions, it authorises the issue of permits for the amount of emissions it would like to see. It does not need information about abatement costs.

Emissions reduction at lowest cost

Different firms have different marginal abatement costs, that is the cost of abating the next unit of pollution. Provided that the permits can be bought and sold, firms that find it cheap and easy to reduce pollution will do so and will sell the permits they do not need to firms that find it difficult to abate pollution. It doesn't matter for this purpose whether the permits are allocated or auctioned, as long as they are tradable. In this way pollution is reduced at the lowest possible cost and trading takes place until all firms have the same marginal abatement cost, equal to the price of the permit. As long as the permits are tradable, the market reveals producers' current understanding of the cost of abatement.

Tradable permits also give flexibility to polluters. For example, if a factory has to close for unscheduled maintenance the owners can sell or lease its permits while it is no longer able to operate; if there is a need to increase production temporarily they can buy or lease permits to allow it to do so.

Carbon capture

Firms that develop the capacity to remove greenhouse gases from the atmosphere (for example by sequestering methane or CO_2) can sell these 'carbon credits' to the Sky Trust.

Future prices

Provided that permits remain valid when traded, they are a form of private property. In the same way that futures markets have grown up for commodities that have not yet been produced, like grain or metals, so they grow up for permits that will be issued in the future. This allows the market to estimate future cost of abatement. This price will guide the strategy of firms and ensure that abatement is carried out flexibly and in a way that is technically efficient.

Enabling true cost pricing

If property rights in the environment are auctioned, the individual or firm that acquires them is paying a cost that is equal to the market rent of the resource. A producer's input cost is a true cost price, and their product or service is itself made available for the true cost price. A consumer pays a true cost price for their use of the environment.

If property rights for time periods in the future can be traded then a futures market will grow up that allows the market to put a true cost price on the right to make use of the environment in the future.

Regulation, taxation and even subsidies may, in some situations, be the best way to protect the environment, but setting true cost prices has the advantage that all individuals and firms have a financial incentive to reduce their impact on the environment. A stewardship economy protects the environment by setting true cost prices through the auction of tradable permits. Tradable emissions permits have the advantage over taxes and charges that they do not require detailed knowledge of abatement costs by the government.

Chapter 12   Fair shares of the natural world

How can an economy provide everyone with fair access to the wealth of the environment? How should we allocate this wealth between current and future generations?

Ownership economy

Allocation of property rights

In an ownership economy, private property rights to land are first allocated by historical acts like purchase, conquest or staking a claim.   When property rights are allocated for extraction or emissions in an ownership economy, they too are generally based on historical claims. Nations with a history of fishing have divided fishing rights amongst themselves, excluding landlocked nations. Rights to emissions permits in ownership economies are often donated ('grandfathered') by governments to firms that have in the past laid claim to these resources by squatting them. And these rights may be indefinite.

To achieve efficient reduction of greenhouse gases, it is essential is to put the right price on emissions. This can be best achieved through issuing the right number of tradable permits, but there are other possible approaches such as setting a tax at the right level. From the perspective of fairness, though, it is critically important how any revenue is distributed and how the permits are allocated at the start of trading.   The effects of different methods of initial allocation of fishing quotas   within European countries demonstrates this. European fish quotas were allocated to national governments by the European Union. Most governments allocated the quotas to the existing fleet and arrange that when a skipper dies or retires his quota goes back into the pool to be re-allocated; in this way the property rights are non-transferable. In the UK, by contrast, the Thatcher government devolved the management of quotas to fish producer-organisations which gave boat-owners the understanding that they could do what they liked with them. Although the legal title to the quotas is unclear, boat owners now buy, sell and lease them. In 1998 the herring and mackerel quotas for one boat were sold for £6 million (Economist 21/11/98:29).

Stewardship economy

Permits for greenhouse gas emissions

The Stern review discusses how permits for greenhouse gas emissions might be allocated amongst different nations. It says, of the proposal that each country's share should be proportional to its population size:

'The notions of the right to climate protection or climate security of future generations and of shared responsibilities in a common world can be combined to assert that, collectively, we have the right only to emit some very small amount of GHGs, equal for all, and that no-one has the right to emit beyond that level without incurring the duty to compensate. We are therefore obliged to pay for the right to emit above that common level. This can be seen as one argument in favour of the 'contract and converge' proposition, whereby 'large emitters' should contract emissions and all individuals in the world should either converge to a common (low) level or pay for the excess (and those below that level could sell rights).

There are problems with this approach, however. One is that this right, while it might seem natural to some, is essentially asserted. It is not clear why a common humanity in a shared world automatically implies that there are equal rights to emit GHGs (however low)... Rights are of great importance in ethics but they should be argued rather than merely asserted. More pragmatically ... action on climate change requires international agreement and this not a proposition likely to gain the necessary approval for it to be widely adopted' (Nicholas Stern 2007:47).

Stewardship does not prescribe who should have access to land and the environment and accepts that some individuals and companies may use more land and resources than others. But it insists that we have equal rights to make use of our environment.

Any proposal for transition to a stewardship economy needs to be able to obtain the necessary broad political support) but if we can agree the ideal of equal rights to emissions, the politics can focus on the practicalities of transition.

Environmental Dividend

A body attempting to manage renewable resources and emissions in a sustainable way needs to ensure that the rate of extraction does not destroy the capacity of the ecosystem to renew itself indefinitely. In a stewardship economy the assumption is that this will be achieved by setting a cap and auctioning permits for extraction and emission, though taxes and regulations may also be used. The revenue from the auctions, or from taxes, is distributed to everyone in equal shares) as an Environmental Dividend. This distribution is easiest to imagine at a national level although ideally it would be global, benefiting not just nations with an historical claim on these environmental goods. If emissions were to be capped at current levels, stewardship results in a transfer of wealth from those responsible for high emissions to those responsible for low emissions. If emissions are reduced year on year, the lowest emitters continue to benefit.

Investing for sustainability

Stocks of assets

The term 'capital' is defined narrowly to refer to a stock of wealth that is used to produce more wealth – that is to say to refer to 'produced capital' in the list below. The term is also used, with qualification, in a broader sense to describe other stocks that contribute to production:

- 'produced capital' (also called 'physical capital') including machinery, equipment, infrastructure, buildings, improvements and other artefacts (used in production)

- 'natural capital' including cropland, grazing land, forests, subsoil resources, fisheries

- 'human capital', which includes:

- individual capital (also called 'human capital') such as knowledge and skills and the ability and willingness to make use of them

- intellectual capital such as knowledge and ways of doing things

- social capital such as relationships, trust and willingness to co-operate and work together for common purposes

- institutional capital, the aspects of governance that contribute to production. Six dimensions have been identified: political stability and absence of violence; rule of law (including property rights and an effective judicial system); government effectiveness; control of corruption; regulatory quality; voice and accountability (D Kaufmann 2005).

- Total capital, in this broader sense, is defined as the Net Present Value of future benefits, i.e., the sum of future streams of revenue, each discounted back to its present value.

Kirk Hamilton (2006) estimated the stocks of natural and produced capital for each country. The residual once these have been subtracted from the total capital is the country's 'intangible capital'. This is mainly human capital but for methodological reasons also includes bits of natural capital that are difficult to value, like fisheries. Over 80 per cent of the differences between the intangible capital of countries can be attributed to a combination of individual human capital (as measured by the proxy measure of 'per capita years of education') and institutional capital (as measured by the proxy measure of 'rule of law').

Measures of wealth creation

Sustainability can be defined as the maintenance of the stock of capital, defined either broadly or narrowly, for future generations Changes in this stock provide a measure or indicator of sustainability.

National accounts traditionally take note of certain sorts of capital but not of others. Gross National Savings is the amount of capital that is produced but not consumed. Net National Savings adjusts this to take account of depreciation. A range of alternative accounting tools have been produced, including 'Genuine National Savings' which starts from the Net National Savings. The value of resource depletion and the damage from pollution to the environment and health is deducted from Net National Savings and the value of operating expenditures on education is added, as this is regarded as investment not consumption (Kirk Hamilton 2007:35). Twenty six out of 120 countries surveyed by the World Bank at the turn of the millennium had negative per capita Genuine National Savings rates (Kirk Hamilton 2007: 169), which indicates that they are engaged in unsustainable development.

The most widely used measure of the performance of an economy is the Gross Domestic Product (GDP), which consists of the sum of consumption, investment, government spending and net exports. It is a measure of the flow of wealth in an economy and is often used as a proxy for development and even for well-being. But its limitations are well rehearsed and highlighted by large-scale natural disasters, where even partial reconstruction leads to a rise in the GDP. More importantly, a country may achieve a rising GDP simply by running down its stocks of wealth – for example by depleting its resources like fisheries.

Investing the revenue

Renewable resources

The challenge when managing renewable resources is to limit their consumption or use to sustainable levels. If this is achieved using the price mechanism, for example by taxation or by auctioning tradable permits, it in terms of efficiency is irrelevant how this revenue is used. However, from the perspective of fairness, it should be used in some way that demonstrably benefits everyone. While it could be used for the collective good, the advantage of distributing it as an equal per capita Environmental Dividend is that it is transparently fair and fully compensates people who pay the true cost price for their purchases provided that these are no more than a fair share of the resource use.

Non-renewable resources

Resource economists deploy Hartwick's Rule (John Hartwick 1977:972) which states that, when exploiting non-renewable natural resources, consumption can be sustained at its highest possible level if all the resource rent from exploiting those resources is invested in produced capital.

This rule meets the requirements of economic sustainability in the weak, though not in the strong, sense. It makes clear that when we use non-renewable natural resources we should use the resource rents to invest in something of lasting benefit to future generations not to fund current consumption. The investment needs to be in produced capital and in human capital, like education and the rule of law, that will continue to support the quality of life of future generations. So, the resource rent should be invested, not distributed as an Environmental Dividend.

Botswana managed its diamond wealth for decades in a way that was consistent with Hartwick's rule and saw an annual rate of GDP growth of over 5 per cent over the same time scale (G Lange & M Wright 2004 in Hamilton p12). The oil-rich nations of Venezuela, Gabon and Trinidad and Tobago would have achieved per capita incomes of around $30,000 (comparable with South Korea and around twice what they actually achieved) if they had followed the rule from 1970 to 2000 (Hamilton (2007:54).

Hartwick's rule relies on a whole range of assumptions – principally that the accounting is accurate, that the natural world has no value other than in production and that human and produced capital can substitute for natural capital. Ultimately of course this substitutability is highly improbable – even if everyone has a PhD and a photocopier we will be in trouble if we run out of topsoil, forest or water.

Hartwick's rule could provide treacherous ground that allows people to justify resource depletion on the grounds that it is counterbalanced by growth in the value of a brand-name or to justify the invasion of an oil-rich country on the grounds that this will bring democracy and so increase social institutional capital.

There is a challenge of how to use the revenue from natural capital as an investment in both a stewardship economy and ownership economies. A stewardship economy does, however provide mechanisms to collect the resource rents and to invest them for the good of all.

Since the atmosphere is not a renewable sink for greenhouse gases, the revenue collected by the Sky Trust should be used according to Hartwick's rule to invest in adaptation to climate change and in developing alternatives to carbon-based fuels. But in view of the opposition to any attempt to put a realistic price on carbon it seems tactically sensible during a prolonged transition period to treat the atmosphere as a renewable resource and distribute the revenue collected by the Sky Trust as an Environmental Dividend. In this way the resource rent could be seen as a mechanism for mitigating climate change rather than a stealth tax.

How quickly to deplete resources

There is another, separate, question about how quickly a country should deplete its resource base. Did the UK choose the right extraction path for its North Sea Oil, or might it have been better to plan to leave some oilfields unexplored until the price of oil rose substantially? Traditional approaches, which have discounted the future at high rates clustered around the long-term real interest rate, are unlikely to apply any sort of restraint on extraction. If development is to be sustainable, the absolute minimum requirement is that resources are not extracted more rapidly than the proceeds can be effectively re-invested.

In a stewardship economy, if a government does want to slow the rate of extraction it can do so either by regulation or by issuing a reduced number of extraction permits for the country for a year and auctioning them. Auctioning permits should ensure that sites and methods used for extraction are the most efficient available, as it is the most efficient extractor who will generate the highest level of profits and so can bid the highest amount. The use of each site for extraction must also be subject to local planning regulations.

Chapter 13   Enclosure or commons?

The few remaining examples of open access regimes or common property, such as the moon and the atmosphere, are at risk of being enclosed becoming privately owned.

Traditional (local) commons

Ownership economy

The **traditional commons** include land in the economic rather than the geographical sense such as the rights to user-managed irrigation systems, groundwater extraction, communal forests, inshore fisheries, grazing and hunting territories.   These are examples of **common-pool resources** – natural or manmade resources from which it is costly (but not impossible) to exclude free-riders (Elinor Ostrom 1990: 30).

Common-pool resources are located in communities in which a defined group of commoners manage the resources as common property.   This requires trade-offs between many different sorts of claim on these resources – grazing, amenity, resource extraction and so on.   There are examples where these institutions have broken down, giving rise to open-access regimes, but there is also evidence that many societies have successfully managed such common-pool resources over long periods of time (Elinor Ostrom 1990: 21).

One feature of the commons that is often not discussed is their exclusion of everyone who is not a commoner.   Commons may be a very fair way of distributing the wealth of that part of the natural world amongst those who live nearby, but this does not take into account the need to share this wealth amongst the whole population.   The commoners of a fishery, for example, are always local and limited to coastal nations so no economic benefit from the fishery finds its way to non-coastal nations.

Stewardship economy

In a stewardship economy all land is held in the form of a Commons Trust which may or may not be under the control of the state. This is unlike a local commons in that the trustees act on behalf of the whole population of a country or even of the whole world.

Private and collective property is held as a use-right from the Commons Trust, as is common property.

Collectively owned (state owned) land is held in stewardship in a stewardship economy, requiring the state to care for the land and to pay stewardship fees for its use. This might seem unnecessary, but even if a proportion of these fees are returned to the state the advantage is that the government has to account for, and give attention to, its use of land. This should ensure that state-owned land is put to good use.

Common property, in the sense of the traditional commons, is also held from the Commons Trust and managed by the commoners. The commoners have a responsibility to care for their commons, for which they are accountable to the Commons Trust, and they have a duty to pay stewardship fees. These fees may be difficult to estimate and may be negative (a subsidy that society is willing to pay for the upkeep of this commons) but they are nevertheless due. When fees are shared with the rest of the population this compensates those who are beyond the local borders of the commons.

Global commons

Ownership economy

The concept of **the commons** has recently been expanded beyond the traditional commons in both scale and scope. Some natural resources can clearly be well managed at a national scale, such as the radio spectrum. And many activities function well as government-created monopolies such as the national grid, utility networks, railways and so on.

Some natural resources are more appropriately considered to be global in scale, such as the atmosphere and satellite orbits.

Common-pool resources at the regional, national, international or global scales may be managed by collective (state) action. Fairly successful examples of these **global commons** include the Montreal protocol that halted the destruction of the ozone layer, at least for a while, and the use of emissions permits (private property rights) to reduce sulphur dioxide emissions.

There is growing support for the proposal that the global commons should be managed as self-organised commons rather than as private or state property (James Quilligan 2009 https://www.kosmosjournal.org/article/people-sharing-resources-toward-a-new-multilateralism-of-the-global-commons). This view derives some of its momentum from our evident failure to use private or collective property rights to tackle climate change; some momentum from a distrust of big government; and some from our awareness that the essential gifts of nature on which our survival depends, like air and water, are being enclosed, taken in to private ownership and made available to us at a price.

The **global commons movement** broadens not just the scale but the scope of what we mean by 'the commons'. http://www.onthecommons.org/about#sthash.OTAGJnjD.dpbs Just as we have seen water and air taken into private property, so we have seen seeds, organisms and genetic information enclosed and privatised. These are all examples of the incursion of intellectual property rights into the cultural commons, and the global commons movement challenges the enclosure of property rights across a wide range of intellectual and cultural areas.

Stewardship economy

A stewardship economy needs Commons Trusts to hold commons in trust on a national or global scale. However, the obvious pitfall when expanding the idea of the commons to a large population of commoners that is that thoughtful conversations amongst commoners are far more challenging. Such conversations may be allocated to trustees, however, as these Trusts do not manage the commons directly. Rather, their role is simply to allocate the resource for which they are responsible and to collect the fees that its users contribute.

It is possible to imagine a Global Sky Trust, for example, that allocates emissions permits and collects the fees. This arrangement would find favour with those who distrust elected governments and believe that the job could be done better by a self-organised commons trust. Those who think that it could be done better by private enterprise would favour a franchising arrangement, while those who feel that the problems of state control are outweighed by the advantages of democratic accountability would want the Sky Trust to be a state body or a body administered by an international body that is either elected directly or appointed by elected national governments.

New enclosures

Enclosure of land to which commoners hold rights has been one of the most significant ways in which fair access to land, and its wealth, has been eroded over the centuries. Traditional commons continue to be eroded. The most significant enclosures taking place at this time are those of open access regimes. Some may be carried out to ensure that a resource that is being squandered because it can be accessed by anyone is used in a way that is both efficient and fair – such as the enclosure of the atmosphere. But others may feel like 'resource grabs' for private benefit – such as the outrageous attempt of an individual to lay claim to the surface of the moon.

Common land in the UK

Ownership

It is worth remembering that enclosure of land to which there are common rights remains a small but significant problem in the UK today. One reason for these enclosures is to generate income by imposing charges (either an ongoing rent or a one-off purchase price) on those who want to use the land and another reason is to acquire privacy by physically excluding the existing commoners.

Stewardship

People might still try to enclose land to which there are common rights, but the presence of a Land Stewardship Trust would make these attempts more visible.

The incentives for enclosure would be much less than in an ownership economy. In a stewardship economy the commoners would from the outset, as stewards, be liable to pay a stewardship fee for their property rights. On enclosure they would pay this rent instead to the proprietor who enclosed the land who would incur the liability to pay the stewardship fee; there would therefore be no financial benefit to be had from the enclosure. If the enclosing steward charged a one-off payment, they would be unlikely to set this above the sum of discounted future rents, which they would be liable to pay – so once again, no financial benefit.

Enclosure to acquire privacy would increase the value of this land, so a steward would compensate the community by paying higher stewardship fees.

The moon

Ownership

The moon provides an example of the dangers of allowing the admissibility of historical claims to contested territory. Who owns the moon? Do countries that have landed equipment on the moon, or landed men on the moon, have claims to territory on the grounds of first occupancy? How much of the moon might they claim? Could we agree that the moon, and beyond, is common property?

In 1980 Dennis M Hope laid claim to the entire surface of the moon by lodging documents with the United Nations and the governments of the USA and USSR. He has made plots available to purchase www.moonestates.com. These claims may seem fanciful, but it is difficult to predict how the lunar surface might be used in the future and how property rights will be handled. It seems a dangerous precedent to allow a group of people to believe that they own the moon. Do we really want to extend the notion of historical ownership rights beyond our own planet?

Stewardship

In a stewardship economy any rights to the moon would come with the duty to make a regular payment to the rest of us as compensation and this liability would increase if the value of those rights increased.

The atmosphere

Ownership

The atmosphere has long been treated as an open access regime, albeit subject to some regulation, and its recent partial enclosure under the United Nations Framework Convention on Climate Change (UNFCCC) has been an attempt to prevent its over-use as a sink for pollutants – particularly for greenhouse gases However, the implementation has been deeply flawed as demonstrated by even one of the most effective regional interventions, the European Emissions Trading Scheme. As noted above, this gifted permits to existing polluters, so effectively legitimising their 'squatters rights'. Many of these gifts were to existing large polluting industries, enabling them to out-compete smaller and potentially greener enterprises.

Stewardship

In a stewardship economy the enclosure of an open access regime would follow a natural course that would be more likely than in an ownership economy to result in a fair and efficient allocation of private property rights and an equal distribution of the benefits to all. Permits create private property rights which are time-limited use-rights not perpetual private ownership. The stewardship proposals are effective, efficient and fair:

Effectiveness

A responsible body. The Sky Trust would be capable of resisting the commercial lobbyists who have denied the anthropogenic contribution to climate change.

Enclosure. Putting an end to a more-or-less open access regime, the Sky Trust would have the responsibility for maintaining an atmosphere free from damaging levels of pollution.

Efficiency

A price for carbon (and other pollutants). The Sky Trust would set a price for carbon, resulting in:

- Reduced demand for goods and services that pollute, as the result of higher prices.

- A stimulus to develop production processes, goods and services that reduce or minimise pollution.

- A reduction in emissions by whichever sections of the economy can achieve them most efficiently.

- Permits rather than taxes. Based on a state decision about acceptable levels of emissions, either permits or taxes could be used to set a price for carbon. If permits are auctioned their price will be set in the market and emitters of greenhouse gases, not governments, decide the most efficient ways to reduce emissions.

Fairness

In an established stewardship economy the revenue from auctioning permits would be used for the benefit of future generations – either to mitigate climate change or to pay for adaptations. This would ensure that our behaviour is sustainable, meeting the needs of the present without compromising the rights of future generations.

Transition

During an indefinite transition period to a stewardship economy, the resource rent – the revenue from taxes or the sale of permits – should be distributed equally, as an Environmental Dividend, to everyone. This is because of the seriousness of the immediate situation and the need for rapid action, and this is the only way to make true cost pricing tolerable and acceptable, particularly for the poor who are hardest hit. The challenges of introducing prices that reflect the true cost of greenhouse gas emissions and changing the behaviours that need to change, is enormous. It is more likely to be achieved if significant numbers of people feel immediate benefit from the proposals.

In summary: Stewardship offers a new way of thinking about property rights to territory (such as the Moon), to the environment (such as the oceans and atmosphere) and to monopolies granted by government (such as intellectual property rights). In each case the underlying principle is that everyone should receive a share of the wealth of the natural world and the rents arising from monopolies created by the state.